# Hate speech and abusive behaviour on social media

## A cross-cultural perspective

**Luiz Valério P. Trindade**

IPIE – International Panel on the Information
Environment, Switzerland

Series in Critical Media Studies

VERNON PRESS

*In the Americas:*
Vernon Press
1000 N West Street, Suite 1200,
Wilmington, Delaware 19801
United States

*In the rest of the world:*
Vernon Press
C/Sancti Espiritu 17,
Malaga, 29006
Spain


Series in Critical Media Studies

Library of Congress Control Number: 2024937431

ISBN: 979-8-8819-0137-0

Also available: 979-8-8819-0024-3 [Hardback]; 979-8-8819-0055-7 [PDF, E-Book]

Cover design by Vernon Press with elements from Freepik.

# Table of contents

# Table of Contents

# List of figures and tables

**Figures**

**Tables**

# Foreword

Receiving an invitation to write a foreword comprises one of the highest honours a professor can receive. More than that, being invited to develop it for Luiz Valério Trindade's book is unique and remarkable. I greatly admire him, with undisputed academic respect and legitimate affection. So, I would like first to express my gratitude for being invited to write these few pages and reiterate that it is a distinction to which I have tried to respond satisfactorily and contribute to introducing a work that undoubtedly will bring invaluable insights and innovative perspectives to readers. Thank you very much, Luiz Valerio!

I consider the author of this book to be one of the most distinctive voices in the study of the social representation of ethnic minorities in mass media, critical analysis of derogatory humour, critical race and ethnic studies, and analysis of hate speech on social media. Indeed, regarding the phenomenon of hateful discourses disseminated on the internet, two of Trindade's previous publications (*No Laughing Matter: Race Joking and Resistance in Brazilian Social Media* and *Discurso de Ódio nas Redes Sociais*), alongside several other publications, offered invaluable contributions to the debate around this phenomenon. In these studies, Trindade conceptualises hate speech as discriminatory ideologies that undermine a person or a social group's value, disrespect, and humiliate them based on attributes such as gender, sexual orientation, religious beliefs, ethnicity, geographical origin or socioeconomic position. He points out that, given the exponential growth rate achieved by social media platforms in the recent past and their ubiquitousness in people's lives, hate speech has shifted from the offline to the digital realm. Within it, racist hate speech has become commonplace and Black women comprise one of the prominent victims of this pernicious practice.

The strength of his analysis, coupled with solid scientific rigour, also reveals how freedom of expression has been exploited as a sort of protective shield by countless haters (i.e., digital criminals), most of whom are not being held accountable for their actions due, first, to the inertia of the state's repressive structure. Secondly, the difficulty of juridically classifying this criminal activity and, finally, due to enduring and ingrained structural racism under which Brazil's national identity was built and still remains a relevant supporting pillar in its social fabric. In addition to these aspects, the instrumentalisation of hate speech and the spread of disinformation online at the service of autocratic political projects cannot be disregarded. Thus, Trindade's critical analysis contributes to illuminating the public debate and fostering constructive change in such a toxic ecosystem.

In the current work, the author analyses, from an innovative cross-cultural perspective, the phenomenon of dissemination of hate speech and bigotry on social media, their adverse societal impacts on individuals, vulnerable social groups, society, and the potential erosion of democratic systems. This way, the work demonstrates the author's academic maturity and the core nature of his research.

Here, Trindade expands his previous studies considerably, analysing not only racist hate speech but also aggressive misogynistic discourses, cyberbullying, revenge porn, fake news, and politically motivated hate speech. In so doing, the book dialogues with the most relevant concerns raised by the academic community, several international organisations and society at large, seeking to understand how the supposedly free territory of the internet has become an echo chamber of the most harmful human feelings.

The author explains that the internet and social media have not created hate speech. However, it is flagrant that content recommended by powerful algorithms, users' constant search for attention and approval through 'likes', and the exploitation of personal data have turned the online environment into an antisocial virtual environment. The shift from a horizontal ecosystem of free speech to a network of reproduction of hierarchical class structures is among the most noticeable side effects of the commercial exploitation of digital platforms.

The work unequivocally points out that hate speech can go beyond mere rhetoric and cause real harm to individuals' lives, stigmatisation of minority groups, ethnic persecution, discrimination, and symbolic and actual physical violence. Amidst it, social cohesion is also affected because, as seen in the global resurgence of authoritarian governments, the internet has been captured as a powerful political tool. Thus, social media platforms have been weaponised at the service of autocrats, many of whom have been elected based on collective fear and hate, and through the systemic dissemination of fake news and disinformation. The combination of these aspects comprises inappropriate 'advisers' for citizens when deciding their vote and who act firmly in the erosion of belief in liberal values and the corrosion of democratic regimes.

Another invaluable contribution of this book is the ample literature review beyond the Anglophone social contexts. Despite recognising the robust and influential relevance of research conducted in these social contexts, Trindade advocates that most of the time, "only studies that explore English-speaking social contexts tend to receive great attention both in academia and beyond. Furthermore, it is a fact that studies addressing the issues of racism and hate speech, for instance, tend to gain greater visibility when exploring events taking place in the US and the UK. Consequently, the research developed in the present book explored literature published in three 'non-hegemonic' languages (Italian, Portuguese and Spanish) in 11 countries to mitigate or reduce this excessive Anglophone concentration. Then, adopting this ample perspective, the present study contributes substantially to the public debate regarding the societal impacts of social media platforms.

In conclusion, I kindly invite you to explore this work fully. I am confident that it is of great interest to established scholars, researchers and students in the discipline of critical social media studies, digital humanities, and sociology, as well as social activists, policymakers, and everyone else who refuses to remain silent before the harm of hate speech and intolerance on social media. Ultimately, I hope we manage to witness the end of all forms of discrimination, hate, intolerance, and racism, both online and offline, well before they turn into something so common that we become unable to remember what life in society was like without them.

**Prof. Dr. Irineu Barreto**
Programa de Mestrado em Direito da Sociedade da Informação
Faculdades Metropolitanas Unidas - FMU

*To Giulia, who was already an essential part of my journey even before she came on board.*

# Acknowledgements

A well-known adage says that 'no man/woman is an island', and I believe the same concept applies to any literary work (fiction or no fiction), meaning that, although writing up is quite a solitary work, it does not mean we accomplish the goal alone. The present study is the outcome of more than two years and a half of hard work, intense reading of dozens and dozens of references in four languages (English, Italian, Portuguese, and Spanish), critical appraisal of all these written materials, and the manuscript's writing up and countless revisions. However, this would not be possible without the invaluable support of many people.

Thus, I would like to thank *Vernon Press* for believing in the project when I submitted my proposal and trusting that I would deliver it within the agreed deadline. It is my second project with them, and I am very grateful for this successful partnership.

I would also like to express my gratitude for the blind reviewers' invaluable time and disposition to read the manuscript and, secondly, for their insightful comments, critical appraisal, and suggestions for improving this work.

A special thanks goes also to my dear friend Prof Irineu Barreto, who kindly accepted my invitation to write the foreword. He did not even think twice when I made the invitation, which has brought me great joy and satisfaction.

Finally, I thank all my friends, colleagues, and family members for their trust in my work and the ability to produce insightful studies.

# Introduction

*"I have never had to face anything that could
overwhelm the native optimism and stubborn
perseverance I was blessed with".*

(Sonia Sotomayor)

Research reveals that, within the past two decades, social media platforms[1] have become a breeding ground for a wide variety of manifestations of online harassment and abuse. Amongst them include the construction and dissemination of racist discourses against  Black[2] people (Chaudhry and Gruzd, 2019; Trindade, 2019), varied forms of hate speech (Shepherd *et al.*, 2015; Jakubowicz *et al.*, 2017), the dissemination of aggressive misogynist discourses (Mantilla, 2013; Jane, 2017), the manifestation of religious intolerance, especially against people professing non-Christian faiths (Awan, 2016; Nogueira, 2020), revenge porn (Bates, 2016; Paulin and Boon, 2021), cyberbullying (Smith *et al.*, 2008; Slonje *et al.*, 2013) and the dissemination of fake news (Allcott and Gentzkow, 2017; Apuke and Omar, 2021; Barreto Junior, 2022).

Speaking of which, it is also relevant to explain that online harassment is regarded as the abusive exploration of modern digital communication technologies with the aim to cause harm to other individuals or vulnerable social groups and the conscious spread of disinformation (Vepsä, 2021). As for hate speech, Tontodimamma et al. (2021, p. 157) define it as "any communication that disparages a person or a group on the basis of some characteristics such as race, colour, ethnicity, gender, sexual orientation, nationality, religion".

---

[1] Currently, the terminologies 'social media platforms' or merely 'social media' are practically consolidated in the literature (including an influential journal in this discipline is called *Social Media + Society*), but previously, there has been a variety of denominations, including Digital Social Networks, OSN (Online Social Network), SNS (Social Network Site or Social Networking Sites), RSD (Redes Sociales Digitales), and SRS (Sites de Redes Sociais).

[2] Should Black be capitalized or not? What about white, should it also be capitalized? This topic has been a subject of debates for many years already. There are voices pro and against its capitalization and both sides have solid arguments to defend their positions. In the present study though, the choice has been made to capitalize Black and not white, in alignment with arguments advocated by authors such as AP (2020), Coleman (2020) and Laws (2020).

The combination of these phenomena has also become the subject of concern for several international organisations such as the United Nations (UN, 2023b; 2023a), the European Union Agency for Fundamental Rights (FRA, 2017), the European Commission against Racism and Intolerance (ECRI, 2018), UNESCO (Gagliardone *et al.*, 2015), the Amnesty International (Amnesty, 2017), among others. Briefly speaking, they not only call the attention to the varied forms of online harassment and abuse but also raise awareness about their adverse societal impacts and demand effective actions from the corporations behind the social media platforms to tackle the abuse.

Furthermore, Tontodimamma *et al.* (2021, p. 174) also argue that "the attention paid to online hate speech by the scientific research community and policy makers is a reaction to the spread of hate speech [...], and to the pressing need to guarantee non-discriminatory access to digital spaces, as well".

Although it is clear that the manifestation of hate speech, racism, misogyny, religious intolerance, xenophobia, etc., was not inaugurated with the emergence of social media platforms in the mid-2000s, it is a fact that this disruptive digital technology has played a decisive role on their spread and amplification. Furthermore, according to the current UN Secretary-General Antonio Guterres, the internet and social media platforms have fuelled hate speech and enabled its instantaneous spread. Additionally, still according to the Secretary, hate speech incites acts of violence, undermines diversity and social cohesion, and threatens the shared values and principles that bind us together (Xinhua, 2022).

Then, in alignment with this overall reflection, according to a study conducted by Trindade (2022), it can be observed that from 2012 onwards, there has been a surge in reported cases of hate speech in many countries, especially soon after Facebook reached the impressive milestone of one billion monthly active users. Indeed, while the large corporations behind major social media platforms claim to be some type of modern democratising forces, studies review that, as a matter of fact, they have instead been playing a decisive role in "mediating and amplifying old and new forms of abuse, hate and discrimination" (Matamoros-Fernandez and Farkas, 2021, p. 206).

Within this context, the body of literature addressing the aforementioned phenomena has also increased considerably in the recent past. Nevertheless, despite the varied types of online harassment and abuse that have reached a global scale, it is noteworthy to highlight that usually, only studies exploring Anglophone social contexts tend to receive significant attention both in academia and beyond. Additionally, in alignment with this reflection, Matamoros-Fernandez and Farkas (2021, p. 209) argue that in the case of studies addressing racism and hate speech on social media, "North America – especially the United States – is by far the most studied geographical context. Europe is the second most studied region, with nearly half of the studies focusing on the United Kingdom".

In the meantime, it should not be disregarded that there is also a robust body of literature examining the same phenomena, however exploring them in other social contexts and published in non-hegemonic languages such as Italian, Portuguese, and Spanish. Nonetheless, despite their relevance and impact, it is possible to observe that they usually lack an equivalent level of international attention. In other words, in practical terms, they remain indefinitely in the condition of 'to be discovered' rather than 'joining the ongoing conversation' in the discipline.

Undeniably, English (spoken by 1.5 billion people worldwide)[3] is an influential language and highly dominant in academia. Indeed, according to Jenkins (2013), English has increasingly become a global linguistic standard in international academic publishing over the past century. Furthermore, according to Crystal (2003), in the 1990s, for example, the journal *Linguistics Abstracts* reviewed the content of over 160 linguistics journals worldwide and discovered that almost 70% of them were published in English, and in the case of physical sciences, the figure had reached nearly 80%.

However, the combination of Italian, Portuguese, and Spanish speakers comprise 873.9 million people worldwide[4], which is considerably representative when compared to English. Consequently, this figure illustrates the relevance and validity of exploring research originally published in these three languages and, more importantly, the social contexts where they have been conducted.

Indeed, in this context, there are other authors who question the power structures that govern global scientific communication regarding impact, visibility and relevance, taking into account that major research databases tend to prioritise just publications in the English language (Sánchez-Tarragó *et al.*, 2015; Bamberg *et al.*, 2022).

Thus, it is considered that the present study contributes to the public debate, reflection, and discussion regarding hate speech on social media. However, adopting an innovative cross-cultural perspective, which explores a sample of studies published in Italian, Portuguese, and Spanish, which, otherwise, tend to remain restricted to a limited audience. This approach contributes to providing a comprehensive understanding of hate speech on social media, moving beyond the predominantly Anglophone focus of previous research. This allows for a more nuanced understanding of how hate speech manifests in different cultural and linguistic contexts.

---

[3] Source: (2022) *Ethnologue.* What are the top 200 most spoken languages? Available from: https://www.ethnologue.com/insights/ethnologue200/

[4] Ibid

Additionally, the development of this study highlights the relevance of taking into consideration cultural and linguistic factors when studying hate speech on social media. By comparing and contrasting findings from different countries and languages, the study sheds light on the ways in which cultural norms and language use shape the manifestation and impact of hate speech online. Ultimately, the present cross-cultural study has the potential to enrich and expand the discipline of critical social media and internet studies by offering a more globally informed, culturally sensitive, and inclusive understanding of hate speech on social media.

## Data and Methodology

The 108 papers analysed in the present study were gathered solely in open-access repositories. The reason behind this approach is twofold. First, relying on open-access databases does not impose any type of barrier to further studies aiming to replicate this research model or expand its scope (e.g., adopting different non-hegemonic languages). Secondly, it aligns with policies adopted by leading international research funding bodies. In this regard, it is possible to notice that the European Commission, through its Horizon funding scheme, clearly states that all projects receiving funding from them are required to make sure that any peer-reviewed journal article published by funded researchers is openly accessible, and free of charge because by sharing research results with the rest of the scientific community, you are contributing to the progress of science in general (EC, 2022).

Indeed, the debate regarding open access and the so-called 'commercial' or 'standard' publishing model has already been addressed by several authors. In this context, May (2019) explains that 'standard' publishing models treat research papers as intellectual properties controlled by publishers and subsequently charging a fee for the academic community to have access to them. On the other hand, May (2019) continues, there has been global campaigns such as Access to Knowledge (A2K) which is concerned with financial constraints, mostly in developing countries limiting their access to knowledge.

While some people in academia might consider that open access publications can eventually trigger lower levels of impact in comparison to 'standard' models of publication, research reveals a diverse picture. First, Antelman (2004) have examined the research impact of open-access articles across four disciplines (philosophy, political science, electrical and electronic engineering, and mathematics). Their study revealed that open-access articles enjoy a greater impact than articles that are not freely available.

A subsequent study conducted by Gaulé and Maystre (2011), adopting a diverse methodological approach, also found a relatively higher level of impact of open-access articles in comparison to "standard' models of publications. Nonetheless, despite a discrete advantage to open-access articles, the authors argue that they did not find very significant differences. But, in any case, they advocate that "in a world of open science, full disclosure of results is a central norm" (Gaulé and Maystre, 2011, p. 11).

Consequently, the sample of papers composing the present study was collected in February and March 2023. To this end, it has been chosen the databases OpenAIRE, SSOAR, ESSPER, and Scielo for identifying the relevant studies and Google Scholar to find out the number of citations of each paper. The adoption of this approach regarding the citations ensured that this data was uniform throughout the whole sample of studies.

According to the description provided on the website, OpenAIRE is one of the world's largest open scholarly record collections, and it receives funding from the European Union's Horizon project. What regards SSOAR (Social Science Open Access Repository) is a database specialising in scholarly articles from the social sciences that is freely accessible on the internet. This project is funded by the German Research Foundation. What concerns ESSPER, it comprises a group of Italian and non-Italian libraries associated with providing services in the field of documentation of economics, social sciences, law, and history. The database includes over 850 titles of Italian academic journals and is open access. Finally, Scielo (established in 1997 in São Paulo, Brazil) comprises an open-access bibliographic database of English, Portuguese, and Spanish publications, with geographical coverage of Latin American countries, Portugal and Spain.

The actual search in the databases mentioned above was performed with the support of a combination of the following equivalent keywords in Italian, Portuguese, and Spanish: a) hate speech, b) racism, c) Facebook, d) Twitter, e) Instagram, f) social media, g) bullying, h) microaggression, i) misogyny, j) bigotry, k) prejudice, l) discrimination, m) discourse, n) internet, o) homophobia, and p) xenophobia.

The criteria adopted in the selection of the studies were the following: 1) pick up only peer-reviewed primary research, meaning that the publication had to be in the form of scholarly paper only, rather than books, dissertations, thesis, or book sections; 2) the study should have been published in Italian, Portuguese, or Spanish; 3) the papers had to be published between 2004 and 2022, taking into account that 2004 marked the establishment of the first social media platforms; and 4) the publication should address at least one social phenomenon associated with or impacted by social media platforms.

This harvesting process led to the identification of 156 relevant publications across the four databases. After careful screening in accordance with the pre-defined selection criteria, this number was reduced to 108, which comprises the actual sampling analysed in the present study. The disregarded publications comprise 22 masters' dissertations, 11 doctoral theses, seven conference proceedings and eight book sections. Finally, it is also relevant to explain that the same methodological approach of harvesting scholarly papers in academic databases with the support of a selection of a combination of keywords and according to specific pre-defined criteria is found in several previous studies, such as Wilson *et al.* (2012), Caers *et al.* (2013), and Matamoros-Fernandez and Farkas (2021).

**Organisation of the book**

The present study is structured into seven main chapters, in addition to an Introduction and the Concluding Thoughts. The **Introduction** is dedicated to providing the reader with the overall context of the research, its motivations, objectives and main contributions. Besides, it also explains the methodological approach adopted in the study and how the book is organised.

**Chapter 1** develops a brief account of the evolution of the internet and social media platforms. However, taking into account that this industry is highly dynamic and in constant evolution, the chapter does not have the ambition to present a comprehensive and definitive history of the digital industry. Instead, it focuses on a selection of key events and milestones to serve first as a contextual background to the reader on what concerns the digital industry, and secondly as a reference. That is, since it consolidates a large amount of information that is usually scattered across several different sources, it offers the benefit of organising them together and relating most of them in a single timeline.

Following the account of the evolution of the internet and social media, **Chapter 2** is dedicated to discussing the antisocial behavioural aspects of social media users that contribute to turn them into toxic virtual environments. To this end, the chapter addresses the concept of colour blindness, online anonymity, the dilemma between hate speech *vs* freedom of expression, and the echo chamber of hate. That is, while Chapter 1 focuses on the digital technologies, this one takes into consideration aspects related to the user of such technologies, and how certain beliefs and behaviour play a decisive role in turning the virtual environment so problematic.

Then, once laid out these two important pillars (i.e., the evolution of internet and social media alongside users' antisocial behavioural aspects), **Chapter 3** has the goal to present the reader with a detailed descriptive statistical analysis of the sample of 108 studies encompassing 11 countries. It also reveals how the studies are distributed within the timeframe 2009-2022, both regarding the language they were published and the level of impact they have reached. Besides, the chapter also explains clearly that the sample of papers gathered for the present study does not have the ambition to represent the whole population and, finally, it also addresses the unintended limitations of the study.

The subsequent **Chapters 4, 5, and 6** are the most robust because they are dedicated to developing a detailed examination of the sample of studies published, respectively, in Portuguese, Spanish, and Italian. To this end, each chapter brings an overview of key data regarding the social media landscape in the represented countries to demonstrate the ubiquitousness of social media in people's lives. Then, following a methodological approach suggested by Jorgensen and Phillips (2002), the papers were examined in an iterative process of interrogation to identify the prevailing themes and, finally, the chapters bring an overview of the social media platforms most examined by researchers in the sample of papers.

Then, **in Chapter 7**, evolving from the reflections and discussions conducted in the preceding chapters (especially 2, 4, 5, and 6), it was possible to develop an innovative explanatory model of the societal impacts of social media platforms. Therefore, weaving together the most relevant concepts, arguments, ideas, and key findings raised in the previous chapters, the model shows that varied types of hate speech are intertwined. Besides, social media plays the pivotal dual role of catalyst and vehicle for the manifestation, dissemination and amplification of this phenomenon, whose victims comprise individuals, vulnerable social groups, society, and democracy. In complement to that, the chapter resorts to the topics addressed in Chapter 2 to discuss the role played by social media users in the dynamic of societal impacts of the digital technology.

That being said, the **Concluding Thoughts** brings the final reflections raised in the study and also advocates that although Anglophone studies tend to receive greater attention in academia and beyond, it has also become clear the existence of a rich and robust body of literature produced in non-hegemonic languages that needs to be known and more recognised by the international academia.

Then, the final remarks present a series of suggestions for future studies, encompassing similar research exploring other non-hegemonic languages, underexplored social media platforms (e.g., Instagram, Telegram, YouTube, WhatsApp, etc.), and powerful artificial intelligence tools such as ChatGPT, Google's Bard and alike.

# Chapter 1

# The internet and social media platforms: A brief history

*"My daily struggle is to be recognised as a subject,
to impose my existence on a society
that insists on denying it".*

(Djamila Ribeiro)

## Introduction

This chapter plays the role of providing supporting contextual background to the cross-cultural analysis of hate speech on social media. Considering that social phenomena are not unidimensional but are instead intertwined with several other elements, events, and variables, the objective is to develop a brief account of the evolution of the internet and social media platforms within the past three decades.

The ambition is not to develop a comprehensive and definitive account of all the events, and naturally, some aspects are not covered here. Instead, the chapter addresses key events and milestones directly and indirectly related to dozens of papers reviewed in the present study.

It starts with the presentation of a timeline of events and milestones that provides the reader with an immediate overview (Figure 1.1) and is followed by a detailed analysis and discussion, weaving them together to serve as a background for the subsequent chapters. Moreover, the timeline also displays the evolution of the number of internet users worldwide, which contributes to unveiling an even clearer picture of the development of the technology industry and its increasing global reach. In summary, this chapter helps to understand how the exponential growth rate of internet and social media has contributed to turn them ubiquitous in people's lives around the world.

## Analysis of the timeline

As it is already common knowledge, the pace of changes and evolution in the digital technology industry is extremely dynamic, and consequently, trying to cover the whole history of this industry can become quite an ambitious task. Thus, within the scope of the present study, it is considered relevant to cover just a selection of some key milestones in the evolution of this industry due to two main reasons. First, to provide the reader with a broader contextual perspective that is relevant within the scope of the present study, and second, to better position the papers analysed in the present study in such a way that it becomes easier to relate them with historical key events and milestones.

Thus, this brief account of the evolution of the internet and social media platforms starts with a timeline, as displayed in Figure 1.1, that allows the immediate visualisation of the array of key events and milestones to be discussed in this chapter.

**Figure 1.1**: Timeline of events in the history of the internet and social media

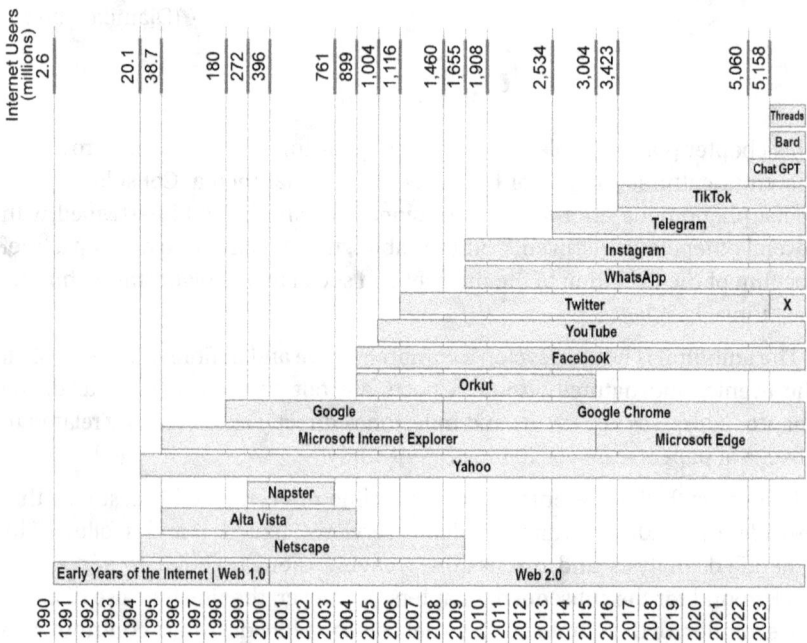

Source: the author, based on BBC (2013), Bertoni (2011), Bhasin (2019), Bonfils (2011), Desjardins (2016), DiNucci (1999), Fildes (2008), Ghoshdr and Chitra (2014), Hughes (2023), Kemp (2023i), Kleinman (2023), Philips (2007), and Ray (2023).

At the outset, **two distinctive milestones** in the evolution of digital technologies are important to highlight: 1) the early years of the internet and 2) the emergence of Web 2.0. **In the early years of the internet in the 1990s** (when there were just 2.6 million users worldwide), it is possible to observe the establishment of several iconic companies and digital products.

Although many people (especially younger generations) might have the impression that web browsers and search engines have been around for a very long time, it was not like that in the early 1990s. In fact, finding websites and any other relevant information was quite difficult, and there was a considerable lack of organisation to make things easier, smoother and more productive for users.

Within this overall scenario, in 1994 (when the number of internet users had grown to 20.1 million worldwide), arrives in the market the innovative Netscape web browser, which very soon would become the leading product in this category, reaching close to 80% of market share in 1996 (Fildes, 2008; Jay, 2008). However, Netscape was still a web browser and not a search engine as people are currently accustomed. Then, also in 1994, it was established Yahoo, which brought some degree of organisation to the content available on the internet by providing users with a series of directories available in several categories (e.g., art, computers, economy, education, entertainment, events, geography, and so forth). The directories were not yet search engines but rather a collection of web links associated with specific categories, quite similar to the old printed bulky *Yellow Pages*[1], and such links were added manually rather than automated. The company became a leading player in this market in such a way that in 2000, its market value was estimated at US$ 125 billion. Years later, in 2016, after losing its leadership position and most of its relevance, the company was bought by Verizon in the US for a fraction of its previous market value (US$ 4.8 billion), then resold in 2021 for US$ 4.25 billion to Global Apollo Management, but is still currently in operation (Desjardins, 2016; Solomon, 2016).

Then, in 1995, a proper search engine arrived, AltaVista, which soon became the world's preferred search engine because it improved considerably users' internet browsing experience. Nonetheless, leadership positions in this industry tend to be quite volatile and susceptible to constant changes. So, also in 1995, Microsoft Corporation (established in 1975) launched its own web browser, Internet Explorer, which benefited greatly from the company's massive market penetration with its Windows operating system.

Some of the ripple effects of these market moves in the following years encompassed the decline of Netscape web browsers that felt from almost 80% of market share in 1996 to less than 1% in 2004. In the meantime, by the end of 1999, Microsoft's Internet Explorer had reached 80% of the market share, and by 2004 rose to more than 90%. Netscape remained in the market for a few more years but did not resist the fierce competition until it ceased its operation permanently in 2008 (Bhasin, 2019).

---

[1] Yellow Pages used to be a printed telephone directory of businesses organized by category rather than in alphabetical order such as in the case of traditional telephone list. They were called this way because they were printed in yellow paper instead of white.

Concurrent with all these events, there was the establishment of Google in 1998 (by that time, the number of internet users had reached 180 million), which brought their efficient algorithm-based search engine to the market. Within just three years of its launch, Google Search had already split the market half-half with AltaVista. From that point forward, Google kept growing and expanding their dominance, so AltaVista ended up being sold to Yahoo in 2003 and shut down a decade later (BBC, 2013; Sullivan, 2013; Islam *et al.*, 2014).

Then, in 2008, when the number of internet users had grown to 1.46 billion, arrived Google Chrome, which also, in a matter of few years, would become the world's preferred internet browser, taking over previous Microsoft's Internet Explorer's leading position in this category (Castro, 2018; Ray, 2023). According to recent figures published by Kemp (2023h), Google Chrome enjoys more than 65% of market share worldwide, while Edge (the current successor of Internet Explorer) has less than 5%.

That being said, the next milestone in the timeline of relevant events in the history of the internet comprises the establishment of Napster in 1999, created by Sean Parker and Shawn Fanning, which comprised a pioneering and highly controversial music-sharing website. It was pioneering because it shattered the global music industry business model of selling music solely through audio CDs and DVDs rather than allowing customers to choose and purchase single tracks of their preferred artists. Moreover, it was controversial because Napster's creators were challenged with copyright infringement by several large record labels (Bertoni, 2011). As a consequence, Napster's original business model (i.e., providing free access to download music tracks) ceased in 2001, and nowadays, it is a paid service similar to Apple iTunes (established in 2001) and Spotify (established in 2006).

However, what is important to say is that the combination of this array of events and technological developments in the 1990s took place in a historical moment regarded as 'the early years of the internet', also called by some authors Web 1.0. In this technological scenario, the communication and interaction among users were relatively limited and categorised as one-to-one, implying that they were basically text-only communication (boyd, 2015)[2].

Within this technological context, several authors believed that the internet would provide society with a virtual environment free of racism, discrimination, misogyny, xenophobia, and so forth (Turkle, 1995; Rheingold, 2000; Lévy, 2001; Poster, 2001; Hansen, 2006). Besides, one of these authors advocated that "by

---

[2] For the sake of clarification, the author danah boyd is written in small letters following the author's own desire as already publicly expressed by her in a number of occasions. To this end, she explains her decision in a blog post available from: https://www.danah.org/name.html.

suspending the automatic ascription of racial signifiers according to visible traits, the online environment can, in a certain sense, be said to subject everyone to what I shall call a 'zero degree' of racial difference" (Hansen, 2006, p. 141). This belief became known as *colour blindness*, which not many years later was challenged and deconstructed by other scholars such as Daniels (2012; 2015), Kettrey and Laster (2014), Yoon (2016) and Pérez (2017). Briefly, these authors advocate that *colour blind* assumptions were made in the context of text-only internet that ceased to exist once the virtual interactions among users became much more dynamic and complex than what was observed in the early stages of the internet.

Then, in the early 2000s, it is possible to notice that the digital technology industry took another leap forward with the development of Web 2.0, which became a big game changer. The term Web 2.0 was coined by DiNucci (1999, p. 32) in an influential article where the author predicted that "the web we know now, which loads into a browser window in essentially static screenfuls, is only an embryo of the web to come. The first glimmerings of Web 2.0 are beginning to appear, and we are just starting to see how that embryo might develop".

Thus, the previous one-to-one communication had evolved to many-to-many communication, meaning that multiple users could simultaneously interact among themselves and construct and disseminate text, images, audio and video content amongst a wide audience (Fuchs, 2008; Castells, 2010). Consequently, the emergence of this technology upgrade was pivotal to the establishment of social media platforms from 2004 onwards because they operate in a powerful network of users who grow exponentially, which could not operate in the context of one-to-one interaction or text-only internet. Therefore, this scenario comprises **the second distinctive milestone** aforementioned. Furthermore, as seen in Figure 1.1, the number of internet users worldwide in the 2000s experienced tremendous growth, which means that entrepreneurs had a huge market potential for their innovative products.

Subsequently, in 2004, it was possible to observe the establishment of some of the first social media platforms (e.g., Orkut and Facebook). Orkut was developed by a Turkish Google engineer named Orkut Büyükkökten and became very successful in India and Brazil. In contrast, Facebook was developed by a group of Harvard University's undergraduate students (Mark Zuckerberg, Eduardo Saverin, Andrew McCollum, Dustin Moskovitz, and Chris Hughes) but later became led by Mark Zuckerberg alone. Initially, Facebook's access was restricted to students of that university, reaching around 3,000 people within three weeks. A month later, it expanded among students from other equally prestigious US universities, such as Columbia, Yale, and Stanford. Then, in 2006, it became global, reaching eight million users.

In 2010, Facebook achieved two important milestones. First, it managed to expand its user base to 400 million people worldwide, equivalent to 20.9% of the number of internet users. Second, it introduced the 'like' button (which is symbolised by a blue thumbs-up icon), which, for the years to come, would not only revolutionise the online advertisement industry but also become a standard feature across all social media platforms. Nowadays, all of them employ either the same 'like' button or similar names or icons for this feature, but in essence, they work in the exact same way and with the same purpose (Phillips, 2007; Bonfils, 2011; Ghoshdr and Chitra, 2014).

Facebook's success rate was so impressive that in 2011, it surpassed Orkut's leading position in Brazil, and in 2014, Google discontinued the service (Google, 2014). Facebook kept growing as a successful business enterprise in such a way that a key person in this achievement was one of Napster's former creators, Sean Parker, who, according to Mark Zuckerberg's words, was "pivotal in helping Facebook transform from a college project into a real company" (Bertoni, 2011; Solon, 2017). Then, a year later, in 2012, after taking over Orkut's leading position in important markets such as India and Brazil with large populations, Facebook reached the impressive mark of one billion monthly active users worldwide (i.e., eight years after it had been established), and by 2017 this figure had doubled (i.e., in just five years). Thus, compared to 3.679 billion internet users worldwide, it means that the proportion of Facebook's user base represented over 54% of this figure in 2017.

Within this thriving technological scenario afforded by the emergence of Web 2.0, it is possible to observe the establishment of several other platforms, such as YouTube in 2005, Twitter in 2006, WhatsApp in 2009, Instagram in 2010, Telegram in 2013, and TikTok in 2016.

Furthermore, another distinctive aspect of this industry is the fact that the arrival of a new competitor might trigger two types of reactions by established players. On the one hand, they can choose to disregard the potential threats brought by the new entrant and trust that their established product(s), leading position, and recognised brand awareness might suffice to sustain their businesses. They might even foresee a certain degree of loss of market share, but probably not big enough to jeopardise their operation and revenue. Some indeed succeed in doing so, while others do not, and Alta Vista, Netscape, Orkut, and Yahoo are good illustrative examples of the embedded risk of this approach.

On the other hand, some companies are unwilling to take such risks and decide instead to offer to buy the new entrant. That has been the case, for example, with Google acquiring YouTube in 2006 (just a year after it landed in the market) for US$ 1.65 billion (Sorkin and Peters, 2006), and Facebook who bought Instagram in 2012 for US$ 1 billion and two years later WhatsApp for

US$ 19 billion (Rusli, 2012; Rushe, 2014). This way not only does the corporation manage to safeguard its leading market position for a much longer period, but it also inhibits the emergence of other competitors. Besides, this strategy maintains the users within their own ecosystem and area of influence.

Corroborating what has been said more than once, the digital industry is extremely dynamic and constant changes are an intrinsic and unstoppable part of the game. Amidst it, as widely covered by the international press, in October 2022, the North American billionaire Elon Musk closed a US$ 44 billion deal to buy Twitter, whose initial offer had been made in April of the same year (Conger and Hirsch, 2022; Lerman, 2022; Murphy *et al.*, 2022). As a consequence of this move, the biggest change in the platform would come just in late July 2023, with Elon Musk's decision to ditch the iconic blue bird logo alongside the name Twitter and replace it with an 'X' (Finighan, 2023; McCallum, 2023; Sherman, 2023)[3]. Then, in early July 2023, Mark Zuckerberg's Meta Corporation launched a rival platform to Twitter called Threads, which triggered around 70 million sign-ups worldwide in the first two days (Chadwick, 2023; Hadero, 2023; Milmo, 2023).

In addition to the numerous branding challenges and associated marketing risks derived from the surprising change of Twitter's name, another relevant aspect is still absent in the numerous critical analyses seen in the mainstream media. It regards what different authors call the phonetic translation for the pronunciation of brand names (Hong *et al.*, 2002; Kelly, 2020). Put it simply, while Twitter and tweets have become easily and meaningfully translated and pronounced across dozens of languages, the same might not happen with a simple 'X'.

Finally, although the topic of artificial intelligence is beyond the scope of the present study, it is relevant to mention that this aspect might represent the next important milestone in the study of the societal impacts of modern digital technologies. By the time this book was being written, technological resources such as ChatGPT and Google's Bard, which rely on advanced Artificial Intelligence technology, and their equivalent competitors are still very recent (Hughes, 2023; Kleinman, 2023; Southern, 2023; Wiggers and Sawers, 2023). Nonetheless, they represent a new avenue of discoveries which will demand further study to enlighten society about their capabilities and potential implications.

---

[3] Despite the announced change, for the sake of consistency with hundreds of published studies, it has been chosen to keep using Twitter throughout the book.

# Chapter 2

# Social media users' antisocial behavioural aspects

*"No one is born hating another person because of the colour of his skin, or his background, or his religion. People must learn to hate, and if they can learn to hate, they can be taught to love, for love comes more naturally to the human heart than its opposite".*

(Nelson Mandela)

## Introduction

While Chapter 1 was dedicated to discussing the evolution of digital technologies (i.e., internet and social media), the present chapter complements that reflection by analysing a series of aspects related to the individual user. In other words, digital technologies are developed having the users as their primary targets, or consumers. Then, what needs to be critically analysed is how the individuals interact with the digital technologies.

Nonetheless, taking into account that, as previously explained in the Introduction chapter, hate speech on social media has become a subject matter of great concern to several social agents; this leads to the need to understand which behavioural aspects contribute to turn digital technologies into antisocial online environments.

To this end, the chapter address four main topics: 1) the concept of colour blindness, 2) the fallacy of online anonymity, 3) the echo chamber of hate, and 4) hate speech *vs* freedom of expression.

The analysis of the concept of colour blindness has the twofold goal of highlighting, first, the fact that online and offline environments are not two separate realities and, secondly, that users carry their values, beliefs and ideologies when they log in. The discussion regarding online anonymity has the purpose to reveal and demystify the common belief among many offenders[1]

---

[1] It is possible to observe that in the literature, there is still a lack of consensus regarding how to call the people who engage in the practice of construction and dissemination of hate speech on social media. It is possible to find terminologies such as 'perpetrators of

that online anonymity might not only shield them from being found, but also to allow them to unleash hate and intolerance.

As with the discussion regarding echo chambers of hate, it helps to understand how individual users might feel empowered once their hateful discourses find echo in like-minded users. One of the adverse consequences of this echo chamber effect comprises the amplification of the reach and harm of hateful discourses on social media. The fourth aspect, hate speech *vs* freedom of expression, represents another controversial debate because, oftentimes, offenders argue that they have the right to freedom of expression to justify their hateful discourses. Then, this important democratic value tends to be conveniently distorted to serve the purpose of shielding them from being held accountable for their actions.

Thus, the discussion around these four topics is important because they contribute to the understanding that as social media platforms have experienced exponential growth rate within the past two decades, as explained in the previous chapter, so has the manifestation of a myriad of online harassment and abuse (especially hate speech) by many users. And the combination of the four aspects discussed in this chapter contribute to turn social media into an antisocial virtual environment. Finally, based on concepts and arguments developed by authors such as Goffman (1959), Picca and Feagin (2007), Pérez (2017) and Eschmann (2023), the chapter explains the main roots behind users' antisocial behaviour on social media. Ultimately, the behaviour is fuelled by a desire to use social media as a sort of backstage to unleash intolerant ideologies but hidden from public scrutiny.

### The myth of colour blindness

As addressed in the previous chapter, in the early stages of the internet, several voices emerged on the international arena, claiming that this technology

---

online hates speech', 'spreaders of hate', and 'aggressors'. Besides, several authors adopt 'hater(s)' as the terminology to represent these individuals. However, although it makes sense, I am not very keen on its use because I understand that it does not fully and accurately portray the individuals. In my point of view, 'hater' conveys the idea of an innate and immutable condition when, in reality, people might learn, be influenced, or be groomed by somebody else to express hate. Consequently, in the present study, I have chosen to adopt 'offender(s)' instead, first, because the way I see it, it does not convey a pre-defined and permanent condition. Moreover, I also consider that for an 'offender' there is room for change of behaviour and attitude, once exposed to clarifying arguments and awareness about the adverse impacts of their attitude, while for 'haters' might not since the sentiment is innate. In any case, it is just a point of view and semantic choice that does not invalidate or compromise any study that has adopted 'hater' or any other terminology.

would provide a colour-blind virtual environment. In other words, the internet would be a largely democratic virtual space, which would allow people to disregard racial differences, misogyny, social inequalities, xenophobic feelings, discrimination and varied forms of intolerance.

In this context, Hansen (2006, p. 141) for example, argued that "by suspending the automatic ascription of racial signifiers according to visible traits, online environments can, in a certain sense, be said to subject everyone to what I shall call 'zero degree' of racial difference". However, a few years later, Daniels (2009) has expressed her disagreement with this argument and said that colour blindness is rather a myth than reality.

Additionally, in a subsequent study, Daniels (2012) has complemented the original argument and explained that the idea behind colour blindness was also flawed because it had been built in the context of a text-only internet, that no longer existed. In fact, what Daniels (2012) argues is that, with the technological evolution, the internet has become a breeding ground for the awakening of 'cybernetic racism', or what she calls 'online white supremacy'. The core idea behind this concept is that "white online supremacy exploits uniquely web-based mechanisms to undermine civil rights and values of racial equality with overtly racist and anti-Semitic speech" (Daniels, 2009, p. 20).

In line with the point of view advocated by Daniels (2009; 2012), other authors such as Kettrey and Laster (2014) also argue that the internet is not a colour-blind territory. The authors assert that, in fact, it is a space in which race and racism are markedly significant, and the results of their studies suggest that, in the US context, "the web is a white space that grants easier access and greater power for white users than users of color" (Kettrey and Laster, 2014, p. 257).

It can be observed that the authors advocate this idea because they understand that white's greater economic and cultural capital equip them with greater access to the internet and digital technologies. Consequently, white Americans have managed to increase their symbolic power and privilege in the online environment, disseminating and reinforcing their own views, values and beliefs about themselves and the 'others'.

Still regarding the lack of neutrality of digital technologies in the dissemination and reinforcement of institutional racism, it is worth highlighting other two recent works. Firstly, Noble (2018) argues that, contrary to popular belief, search engines such as Google, Bing, and alike do not offer an egalitarian virtual space for the emergence of varied forms of ideas, identities and values. In fact, adds the author, discrimination comprises a serious problem. The combination of private interests in the promotion of certain websites, as well as the monopolising status of a small number of search engines, leads to biased search results that privilege whiteness over blackness, especially disadvantaging Black women.

Secondly, and in alignment with the work just mentioned, Silva (2019; 2022) defends the concept of 'algorithmic racism'. According to the author, this construct is defined as interfaces and automated systems, such as social media platforms and search engines, that not only reinforce, but also hide racist dynamics in societies where they are employed and widely disseminated.

Along these lines, several studies reveal that, at the same time that social media has grown in reach, popularity and revenue over the past two decades, it has also become a breeding ground for the dissemination of hate speech, discrimination, intolerance and a wide variety of inappropriate content. Indeed, it can be observed that social media have become a virtual arena that allows people to distil all kinds of racist, misogynistic and discriminatory discourses against different social groups. This digital technology has given them the ability not only to construct hate speech, but also to disseminate it to a wide audience and instantly.

In other words, social media platforms have enabled the amplification of latent hate speech. Thus, when people post or share hate speech on social media, they are in fact, reinforcing and reiterating a series of deep-rooted discriminatory ideologies in relation to the object of their attack. This reflection is important because it helps us understand that people's attitudes in the virtual environment are not dissociated from the offline environment in such a way that their values, beliefs and ideologies are also mirrored or replicated on social media.

Furthermore, as argued by Kolko *et al.* (2000, p. 5) in the case of racism in the online environment, "all of us who spend time online are already shaped by the ways in which race matters offline, and we cannot help but bring our own knowledge, experiences, and values with us when we log on". Consequently, this reflection not only reinforces the perception of colour blindness as a myth but also contributes to understand that offenders replicate online the same discriminatory and intolerant ideologies nurtured offline.

### The fallacy of online anonymity

According to Caers *et al.* (2013), on most social media platforms, the process to setting up an account is very simple. Usually, what is required is to be over 13 years old, to provide some basic personal information (such as name, date of birth, gender and a valid email address) and create a password. However, Halfeld (2013) explains that there are no technical barriers that would prevent a user from setting up an account with an alias or nickname instead of their real name to remain anonymous in their communications.

In this sense, anonymity is understood as "a condition where the sender or source of information is absent or not identifiable" (Misoch, 2015, p. 536). But it is important to remember that anonymity in the online environment does not necessarily imply something negative. Among the benefits of anonymity, Kling *et al.* (1999) indicate the following: a) it can be useful in the development of investigative journalistic projects; b) it can allow the communication of sensitive issues without the source being exposed; c) it can support confidential police investigations; d) it can be very useful for people who needs specialised advice in a confidential manner; and e) it can contribute to avoid political persecution.

On the other hand, there is also the malicious use of the anonymity feature in the online environment, and studies point to the following: a) the dissemination of spam, b) the practice of intentionally misleading and fraudulent business and financial transactions, c) the spread of hateful messages, d) offence and defamation, and e) dissemination of fake news, among other illegal activities. Therefore, what Kling *et al.* (1999) reveals is that anonymity in the online environment can have a clear, well-defined and justifiable purpose, but it can also open a huge avenue for a myriad of very questionable attitudes and practices.

In fact, the technological evolution of the internet from text-only to a more dynamic environment, as explained in Chapter 1, has also allowed online anonymity to be used to disguise a series of attitudes and behaviour that not necessarily the person would perform in conventional social contexts (i.e., offline).

In this regard, there is an interesting study conducted by Hughey and Daniels (2013) where the authors have examined online versions of a series of eight US newspapers from the early 2000s, which began to allow readers to comment on some of their news articles. The market strategy behind this initiative was an attempt by the newspapers to engage the public with the available content and also to attract potential new readers, who could eventually become paid subscribers.

Nonetheless, what the study revealed is the fact that the newspaper editors did not foresee and were also unprepared to deal with a surge in offence and racist comments, even when the news articles had no correlation with racial issues. In this particular study, the authors state that they were only interested in racist language and, as a result, it is not possible to understand whether the news articles also triggered other types of comments such as misogynistic, xenophobic and so on.

Yet, what can be inferred from the study conducted by Hughey and Daniels (2013) is that, taking into account that online newspapers had allowed anonymous comments, many people conveniently hid behind this feature to disseminate rude comments, fearless of any restriction, disrespecting social conventions and also fearless of being blocked by the newspapers. Still according to the authors, this was a very challenging scenario for the newspapers editors, who were left with just three possible courses of actions: 1) not allowing comments or allowing them only in selected articles; 2) no allowing anonymous comments and require some sort of registration and identity confirmation; or 3) adopt a content moderator prior to the publication of the comments.

Consequently, it can be observed that online anonymity can act as a sort of shield, conveniently 'protecting' (or preventing) people from being immediately identified and allowing them to speak their mind without any type of restriction or filter. Furthermore, it is problematic to notice that the technical capability of creating anonymous profiles on social media might also contribute to trigger on many users the fallacious belief that they cannot be identified and located. And this also makes them feel 'empowered' to express hate without restraint or reservation against any person or social group.

Nonetheless, contrary to the belief that people can say whatever they want in the online environment because there would be no legal consequences, it is a flawed assumption. That is said because research reveals that there are technical resources that allow not only the identification of individual users but also their exact location (Egelman *et al.*, 2016; Deligiannis *et al.*, 2018; Rusert *et al.*, 2019). Furthermore, there is also evidence revealing that the offenders' belief in the pseudo-protective power granted by anonymity is shattered once their attitude becomes the subject of news articles. In this context, Trindade (2018) has identified that, in such circumstances, offenders take the following measures: a) delete the offensive post, b) change the status of their social media accounts from public to private, c) delete the account in the social media platform, and d) claim that the post was meant to be a 'harmless' joke.

Therefore, these attitudes contribute to reinforce the perception that their belief in the power of anonymity was not as strong as initially believed, and also that they had at least some degree of understanding of the inappropriateness of their behaviour. Otherwise, there would be no need to take the defensive measures just mentioned.

### Social media and echo chambers of hate

According to Larsson (2015), Facebook (and by default, also many other social media platforms) can be characterized according to what is called four modes of communication: 1) *broadcasting*, what means the capacity of posting messages and varied forms of content; 2) *redistribution*, what represents the capacity of sharing and disseminating content across a network of contacts; 3) *interaction*, what means commenting on a specific post and expressing opinions; and 4) *acknowledge*, what, in the context of Facebook, is better known as 'like' and indicated by a blue thumbs-up icon, which is also the company's official logo. In January 2016, the corporation has expanded the range of possibilities for users to interact with the content on the platform by adding five new icons called 'Reaction', allowing people to express 'love', 'sadness', 'astonishment', 'anger' and 'laughter' (Guardian, 2016; Vilicic and Beer, 2016).

However, since these new icons are, in fact, just simply variations of the 'like' function, their incorporation did not change the aforementioned four modes of communication. Indeed, based in this reflection, it can be inferred that, when it comes to hateful content published on Facebook, it goes through the following stages: a) posting (i.e., a person or group of individuals willing to convey discriminatory and intolerant ideologies), b) redistribution or sharing of content by other people with converging points of view, c) comments to the post, and d) 'like', which can be interpreted as a sign of approval or endorsement of the specific content, and also represents an easily recognisable form of engagement triggered by the content (Trindade, 2018).

Briefly speaking, this dynamic of creating (posting), disseminating (sharing), commenting and endorsing ('liking') hateful content means that Facebook facilitates the unrestricted circulation of these discourses and also becomes "a sphere that enables new forms of cultural expression and content consumption" (Boxman-Shabtai and Shifman, 2015, p. 523). And why is it important to understand this mechanism? Because Facebook created this trend or 'industry standard', in such a way that all other platforms that came after them have adopted exactly the same mechanism or logic. In the case of Twitter, for example, it is called 'retweeting' instead of 'sharing'. On Instagram, instead of a thumbs-up icon, there is a heart, while on YouTube, there are thumbs-up and thumbs-down to express the engagement with the content. But, most importantly, the set of functionalities of these social media platforms have allowed people to share a myriad of discriminatory and intolerant ideologies and thus disseminate and reinforce their discourses in ways, speed and reach never seen before in many social contexts.

However, as previously said, not only Facebook, but all other social media platforms are based on powerful network connections. These networks are made up of thousands and even millions of interconnected nodes, which are, in fact, the active users. Therefore, it is possible to see that the more users are connected to a particular content provider (or influential user), the greater the capacity to disseminate content generated by that particular 'influencer'.

Besides, this amplification capacity does not happen in linear way with incremental increases but rather exponential and accelerated. Indeed, Cann *et al.* (2011) explain that a network comprised of just five users can establish a total of ten connections between them. If this network expands to ten users, they will be able to establish up to 45 connections between them. Finally, a network with 15 users is capable of establishing 105 connections.

Therefore, what is being highlighted is social media's enormous capacity for amplifying hate speech. In other words, they can be used as powerful echo chambers, instantly conveying and disseminating multiple discriminatory and intolerant ideologies for a long period of time as an endless echo in the online environment. Speaking of which, Justwan *et al.* (2018, p. 2) explain that echo chambers are "ideologically congruent and homogenous environments in which political views are not debated but instead reinforced and amplified".

Indeed, in this context, research reveals that hateful discourses fostered on social media is capable of keep engaging new and recurring users for up to three years after the original publication of the post, which reinforces the existence of this echo chamber effect of like-minded users expressing their congruent discriminatory and intolerant ideologies (Trindade, 2018; 2020b).

One of the adverse impacts of this practice comprises the amplification of the harm and psychological distress caused to the victims. Finally, it is also important to highlight that oftentimes hateful discourses tend to circulate across different platforms since, in many cases, users have accounts on multiple social media. Furthermore, in the case of Facebook corporation, which in 2021 was renamed Meta, also owns Instagram and WhatsApp, which allows a high degree of technological integration among the platforms and, consequently, it becomes easier for this type of content to circulate across them.

### Hate speech *vs* Freedom of expression

It is possible to observe that on several occasions, freedom of expression tends to be used as a sort of protective shield by individuals who engage in the practice of construction and dissemination of hate speech on social media. Indeed, the reflection concerning the contrasting relation between hate speech *vs* freedom of expression also leads to reflections regarding the topic of internet regulation. This topic has been the subject of international debates for a long time, with divergent viewpoints regarding the level of control or supervision of content published and disseminated on the internet and also different approaches adopted in many countries.

Given this scenario, the international organisation Internet Society argues that "the internet consists of an open platform for innovation and sharing of ideas", and that "it cannot be regulated in a top-down manner, but its governance should be based on processes that are inclusive and driven by consensus" (Society, 2016, p. 1). Similar to this viewpoint, Delacourt (1997) is another voice advocating a non-regulation approach. However, the author recognises that possible government control would be "the ideal alternative

[but] it is no longer realistic in light of the strength of political forces aligned against it" (Delacourt, 1997, p. 234). On the opposite side of this debate, Hughes (2015, p. 1) argues that "a clear regulatory framework is fundamental for the promotion and protection of civil rights in the digital context.

Yet, despite these invaluable debates is still possible to notice the existence of a sensitive debate confronting freedom of expression *vs* disrespect for social conventions (i.e., hate speech). In other words, what is observed is that people who are engaged in the practice of construction and dissemination of hate speech on the internet in general, and especially on social media, claim that they have the constitutional right to freedom of expression and that the initiative to question what they say or write online represents censorship. However, the flaw embedded in this argument is the fact that freedom of expression does not exempt people from civil responsibilities and compliance with social norms, conventions and legal regulations.

Consequently, as explained by authors such as Rossini *et al.* (2015), Dunham (2016) and Kelly *et al.* (2016), freedom of expression online and offline comprises a fundamental component of democratic societies. Nonetheless, many people who engage in abusive behaviour online often try to hide themselves behind this argument as a sort of convenient escape route or excuse.

In this context, according to Daniels (2009, p. 163), in Germany, for example, "freedom of speech is a central tenet of their view of democracy, and their interpretation of this right includes bans on certain forms of white supremacy online". The author also adds that this debate is relevant and necessary in different social contexts, because words are embedded with power and have the ability to engage people either in pleasant or unpleasant thoughts, feelings, ideas and beliefs.

Therefore, on the one hand, freedom of expression represents an important democratic tool that contributes to people's empowerment. On the other hand, it cannot be ignored that, with regard to the practice of construction and dissemination of hate speech, freedom of expression does not exempt users from their responsibilities in complying with norms, social conventions and the legal framework of their countries.

### Understanding online antisocial behaviour

The examination of the aforementioned four behavioural aspects allows the establishment of conceptual parallels with previous works such as Pérez (2017) and Eschmann (2023), because both authors argue that while people refrain from manifesting discriminatory behaviour in public, they do not feel restrained to do so in private (and naturally, social media does collaborate with that).

In this sense, Pérez (2017, p. 956) argues that "while overt racist discourse has declined from public view since the Civil Rights era, it continues to reside in private contexts or has become codded and covert in public". Besides, according to Eschmann (2023), it can be said that in the case of online racism, the hood of intolerance (i.e., a symbolic mask), white supremacy, misogyny, etc., just comes off when people are seated before a computer screen, and their true face is then displayed.

Furthermore, life in society implies the acceptance of its structure of social control, norms of conviviality, and conventions (written and institutionalised and/or passed on by oral tradition). Amidst it, individuals' agency can conform to them, propose changes and improvements through democratic institutions and mechanisms, or engage in conflicting deviant behaviour. That is, they clash with the established norms of conviviality. Thus, antisocial behavioural aspects addressed in the present chapter fall within this description, given that they subvert and disregard the social conventions both in the private and in the public domain. Indeed, taking into consideration that performing intolerant behaviour in public is usually considered inconvenient or unacceptable, social media has allowed them to flourish in the private realm of the online environment.

Within it, is also interesting to observe that in many circumstances, individuals who engage in online bigotry claim that, in reality, they are not purposely offending others but rather exercising their right to freedom of expression, as previously addressed. Moreover, they also say that those who criticise them are members of a sort of 'politically correct patrol' or people who cannot take or understand jokes.

Evolving from these reflections, a possible theoretical explanation to better understand online antisocial behaviour is found in Goffman's (1959) seminal studies, which offers invaluable insights into individuals and social groups' everyday performances in private and public. Although the study is relatively old, the conceptualisation developed by the author still remains relevant and influential in such a way that the International Sociological Association has praised this work as one of the ten most important sociological books of the twentieth century[2]. Then, according to Goffman (1959), individuals present different characters and perform them according to the circumstances, like theatre actors on stage.

Amidst it, following the analogy of a theatre, the author suggests that the context where individuals perform their roles is divided into frontstage and

---

[2] Source: ISA - International Sociological Association: Books of the XX Century. Available from: https://www.isa-sociology.org/en/about-isa/history-of-isa/books-of-the-xx-century

backstage. Briefly speaking, the frontstage represents the visible aspects of an individual's behaviour and how they interact in society according to the established rules, values, conventions, and regulations. On the other hand, the backstage symbolises the behaviour and attitudes not seen by the 'audience'. They are somehow kept hidden, disguised or dissimulated from other people's eyes and public scrutiny.

Indeed, this reflection coalesces with the concept of *backstage of racism*, as coined by Picca and Feagin (2007, p. 91), in the sense that it represents "a space that is safe from certain frontstage expectations about interpersonal politeness of racial matters". That is, while in the frontstage, people are often aware that explicit racist manifestations are inappropriate, in the protected backstage realm, however, openly racist comments can circulate. Thus, the authors continue, "the backstage is a safe zone in which to perpetuate and perform racist jokes and [depreciative] humorous comments that seem essential to sustaining modern racism" (Picca and Feagin, 2007, p. 96). Consequently, the backstage comprises a comfortable and convenient atmosphere for the open manifestation of a variety of online harassment and abuse.

Then, in alignment with what has been analysed in the present chapter, it is possible to notice that many people who engage in the practice of fostering offence online tend to believe that the digital technology affords them a certain degree of anonymity, which allows them to unleash all sorts of hateful discourses freely. As such, they also believe that anonymity shields them from being held accountable for their attitudes and, as a consequence, they feel completely at ease and comfortable manifesting this sort of discourse.

Thus, following Goffman's (1959) and Picca and Feagin's (2007) argumentation, it can be said that social media afford or facilitate people to display and perform their backstage behaviour in full in the online environment, while offline, it remains hidden and only the frontstage acting is shown because it does not clash or confront with the established social structure. Besides, this reflection also resonates with the arguments defended by Pérez (2017) and Eschmann (2023) as aforementioned.

Nevertheless, while the frontstage acting performances are meant to be publicly displayed, the backstage performances are not, and even less being openly or publicly associated with specific 'actors'. Thus, it means that if, by any chance, a backstage performance becomes public, the social actor responsible for it does not want the recognition of this association. However, then, what happens when this logic is disrupted?

Well, the 'actor' strives to dissociate themselves from the performance and returns to a state or condition of anonymity. In the context of social media platforms, this pattern is very clear because, as seen in the section *The fallacy of online anonymity*, the moment that cases of online bigotry and hate speech become the subject of news articles and, consequently, what was supposed to remain in the backstage comes forward, the 'actor' (i.e., the offender) engages in one or more of the following initiatives: 1) claim that the post was meant to be a 'harmless' joke, 2) delete the post, 3) delete the account in the social media platform, and 4) change the status of their account from public to private.

Consequently, these initiatives contribute to corroborating the pattern mentioned above of 'actors' (i.e., offenders) striving to dissociate themselves from their questionable performances and trying to return to anonymity, which is the main characteristic of backstage performances, where the 'audience' (i.e., society) is not supposed to see what they do.

Then, what can be inferred is that this sort of attitude does substantiate the belief in full anonymity; otherwise, there would be no need to take those measures. In other words, the offenders' belief in the power of online anonymity shielding them from facing the consequences of their attitudes is flawed and fallacious because once they become exposed, all the previous bravery to unleash aggressive discourses fades away.

Consequently, since it was something to be ashamed of, so they attempted to retrieve it to backstage. In fact, Goffman (1959) argues that when the boundaries between the frontstage and backstage behaviour are inadvertently transgressed, it becomes very embarrassing for the 'actor'.

Therefore, while in most circumstances, it might not be appropriate or convenient to perform racism, xenophobia, misogyny, religious intolerance, etc., in the 'front stage', social media becomes a sort of 'digital backstage' that allows people to unleash their hate and intolerance in full freely.

# Chapter 3

# Sample of cross-cultural studies: Descriptive analysis

> *"Gender equality is more than a goal in itself. It is a precondition for meeting the challenge of reducing poverty, promoting sustainable development and building good governance".*
>
> (Kofi Annan)

## Introduction

Briefly speaking, the previous two chapters have addressed, respectively, the evolution of the digital technology industry, and social media users' behavioural aspects that can turn social media into an antisocial virtual environment. Thus, having presented these two important pillars, the present chapter is dedicated to describing the selection of 108 scholarly papers gathered for the development of the cross-cultural analysis, that will be addressed in greater detail in the subsequent chapters 4, 5 and 6.

Hence, at this point, it is relevant to explain and clarify that the inferences developed in the present chapter are restricted to the sample of papers gathered for this study, and do not have the ambition to represent the whole population of scholarly papers published in the three languages. Besides, since the methodological approach adopted in this study was to work solely with open access publications, this decision also impacts in the descriptive analysis.

Nonetheless, although this aspect represents an inherent unintentional limitation of the study, it is considered that it does not jeopardise the reflections raised due to two main reasons. First, because, as previously mentioned, the analysis is restricted to the sample of studies. Secondly, because several other similar previous studies have developed descriptive statistical analysis to explain their findings based also on a limited sample of papers (e.g., Wilson *et al.*, 2012; Caers *et al.*, 2013; Matamoros-Fernandez and Farkas, 2021).

Consequently, the chapter addresses four main topics as follows: 1) an overview of the countries represented in the sample, 2) the evolution of publications according to the languages, 3) evolution of publications in combination with the number of citations, and 4) the impact of publications according to the language.

### Descriptive statistical analysis

As previously explained in the introductory chapter, it has been identified a total of 108 scholarly articles published in Italian, Portuguese, and Spanish in the timeframe 2009-2022. However, more than a longitudinal literature review, the aim here is to provide the reader with a broader geographical perspective of the varied forms of online harassment and abuse on social media.

Indeed, in this regard, Matamoros-Fernandez and Farkas (2021) explain that the common exclusion of non-English articles in review studies often limits the geo-linguistic reach of this kind of research.

Consequently, the first distinctive aspect revealed in the sample of selected papers comprises the large geographical coverage represented by 11 countries and two cross-cultural studies, as displayed in Figure 3.1.

**Figure 3.1**: Countries and number of studies in the sample

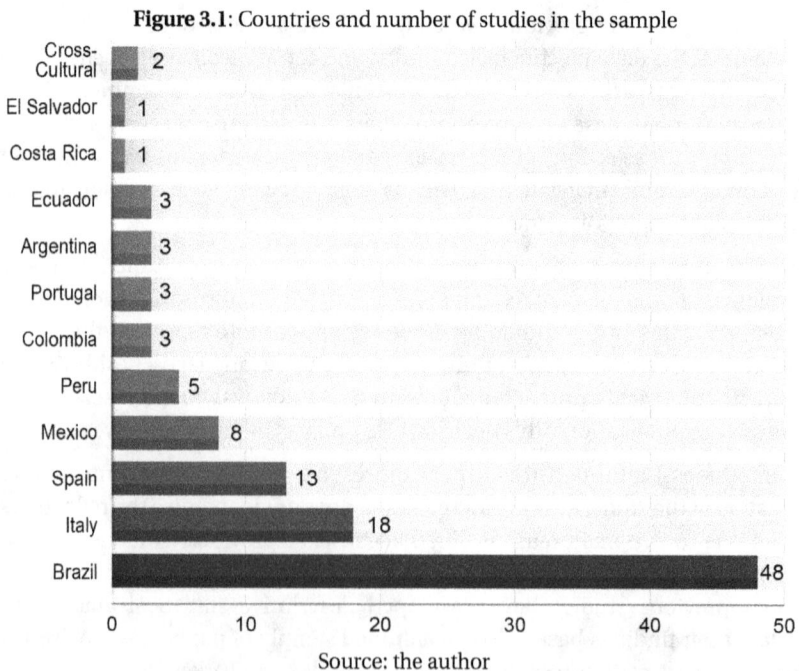

Source: the author

The results show that the majority of the papers were published in Brazil, or they address the Brazilian social context broadly speaking (48 out of 108, or 44.4% of the sample), followed by Italy with 18 studies (16.7% of the sample), Spain with 13 studies (12% of the sample), and Mexico with eight studies (7.4%

of the sample). Nevertheless, despite this large predominance of a single country in the sample, when the data is analysed from the perspective of the languages in which they were published, it is possible to notice the following picture: a) Portuguese accounts for 51 studies (47.2% of the sample), b) Spanish accounts for 39 studies (36.1% of the sample), and c) Italian accounts for 18 studies or 16.7% of the sample.

These figures are important because they contrast greatly with the findings revealed by Matamoros-Fernandez and Farkas (2021), where the authors reviewed 104 English-only papers and identified that 44.23% of their sample addressed North America (i.e., mostly Canada and the US), while just 0.96% comprised South America (i.e., Portuguese and Spanish-speaking countries).

Then, another distinctive aspect that it was possible to observe comprises a large concentration of studies published between 2016 and 2021 (see Figure 3.2). A possible explanation for this concentration comprises the significant increase in reported cases of hate speech on social media platforms, especially after 2012, when Facebook reached the impressive milestone of one billion monthly active users, as explained by Trindade (2022). Thus, it can be implied that this scenario might have contributed to triggering the interest of social scientists and then leading towards several publications in the subsequent years.

**Figure 3.2**: Evolution of publications over time according to the languages

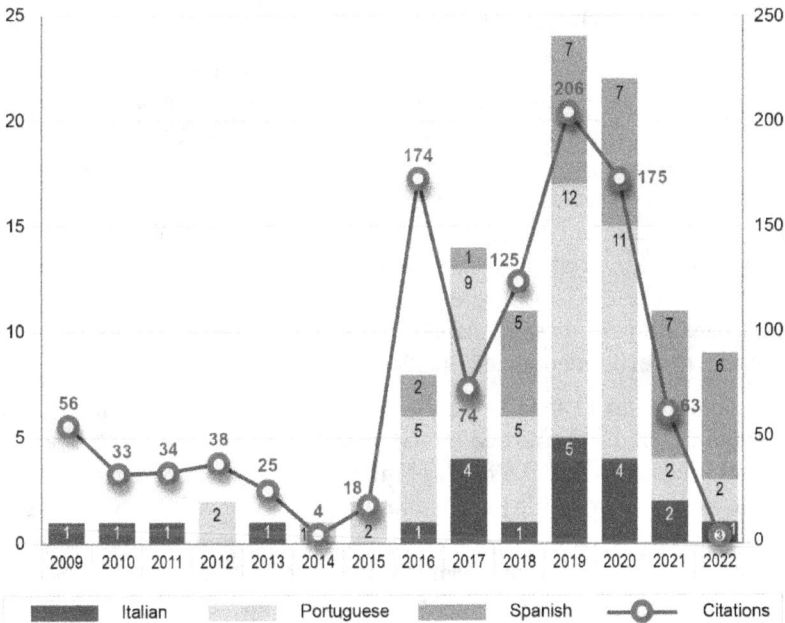

Source: the author.

On the other hand, while from 2009 to 2015, very few studies were published; apparently, in 2022, there was also a considerable decline after several years of large productivity. Nonetheless, an important variable to consider in the reduction of published articles in the timeframe 2020-2022 refers to the long periods of lockdown and restrictions in many countries due to the COVID-19 pandemic, especially in 2020 and 2021. Although the reported cases of hate speech and bigotry on social media during this period did not show any sign of reduction, new studies will probably be published and indexed soon.

Moreover, in line with this hypothesis, recent studies have argued that the COVID-19 pandemic may have impacted the scientific production of non-COVID-19 research, most probably due to reduced editorial capacity. Additionally, different authors also argue that COVID-19 has disrupted research worldwide, leading to lost research time and increased anxiety among researchers (Forti *et al.*, 2021; Raynaud *et al.*, 2021; Suart *et al.*, 2022).

Besides, in the case of 2022, it cannot be disregarded that since in most journals, the time span between the submission of papers and their actual publication usually takes several months (sometimes even a year or slightly more), the results displayed in Figure 3.2 will likely change and become significantly different in the near future. Another distinctive aspect that calls one's attention to the sample of papers comprises the fact that while publications in Spanish and Portuguese were already available since 2009, the ones in Italian have been published just from 2016 onwards.

At first glance, this picture could, eventually, lead to the interpretation that the subject matter of varied types of online harassment and abuse did not raise concerns among Italian researchers. However, this is not the case. First, it cannot be disregarded that the present study examines only open-access scholarly articles, and, as a consequence, this methodological choice influences the sample. Furthermore, several Italian authors have published in English prior to 2016 (e.g., Giglietto *et al.*, 2012; Lovari and Giglietto, 2012; Mascheroni and Mattoni, 2013). Thus, it is fair to say that Figure 3.2 does not tell the full story regarding studies published in Italian. However, it is an indirect consequence of unintentional limitations of the study.

In continuation to the descriptive analysis, another important appraisal refers to the impact generated by the publications. In this case, the level of impact is considered as the result of the number of citations reached by the paper, as already explained in the introduction chapter. This metric can be obtained by different means, such as directly from the journal where the paper was originally published or major databases (e.g., Web of Science, Scopus, ProQuest, etc.). Nevertheless, since one of the methodological criteria adopted in the present study was to work solely with open-access publications, the level of impact was examined using Google Scholar.

Having explained this distinctive aspect, it can be noticed that although the impact reached by publications in the three languages (Italian, Portuguese, and Spanish) usually tend to be lower than publications in English, even so, they have reached considerable results (see Figure 3.3).

**Figure 3.3**: Evolution of publications and the combined number of citations over time

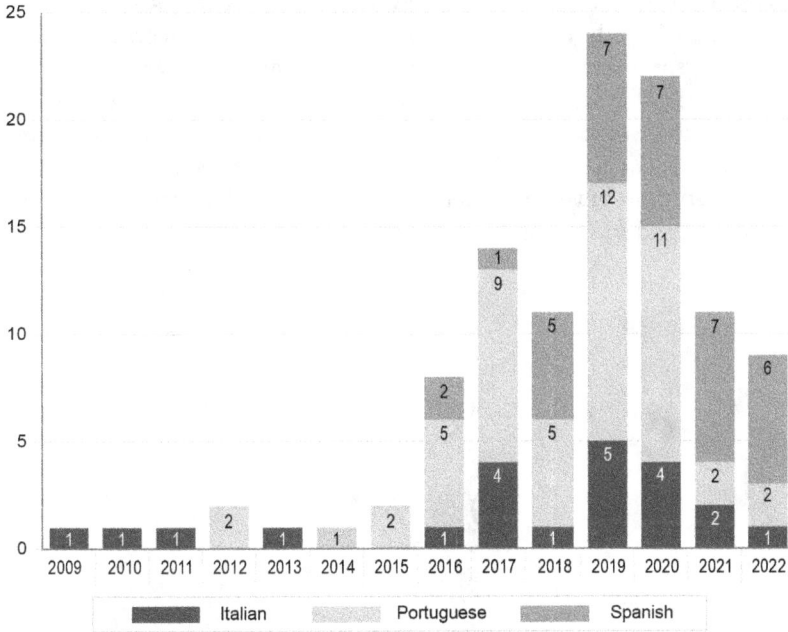

Source: the author.

It is also possible to notice that although in the period 2009-2015, there were very few publications, even so, they have reached a considerable impact of 208 citations in total for just nine articles, representing an average of 23 citations per article.

In the period that concentrates more studies (2016-2021), it is understandable that combined, they have generated more impact, and the highlights are 2016, when just eight papers received 174 citations (an average of almost 21 citations per paper), and 2019 with the highest number of combined citations (206) but diluted across 24 articles what represents and an average of just approximately nine citations per article.

What concerns the decline in the number of citations observed in 2021 and 2022, they should not be interpreted as a reduction in impact. Instead, they are explained by the fact that it takes a considerable time to publish new studies citing the papers released in 2021 and 2022 and also for Google Scholar's algorithms to capture and register the data. Nonetheless, the same previous explanation regarding the temporary reduction in the number of published papers in this period applies here in such a way that these figures are certainly subjected to changes in the near future.

All things considered, what the descriptive analysis reveals are two main aspects. First, very different from previous studies exploring solely articles published in English, the sample gathered for the present research brings a broader perspective and contributes to filling a gap in the literature. Second, although the publications in languages other than English might not enjoy an equivalent level of exposition, which could contribute to achieving higher levels of impact, they still manage to generate a considerable number of citations, and this is very representative in terms of their capacity to create engagement and add a contribution to the discipline of social media studies.

**Figure 3.4**: Impact of publications according to the language

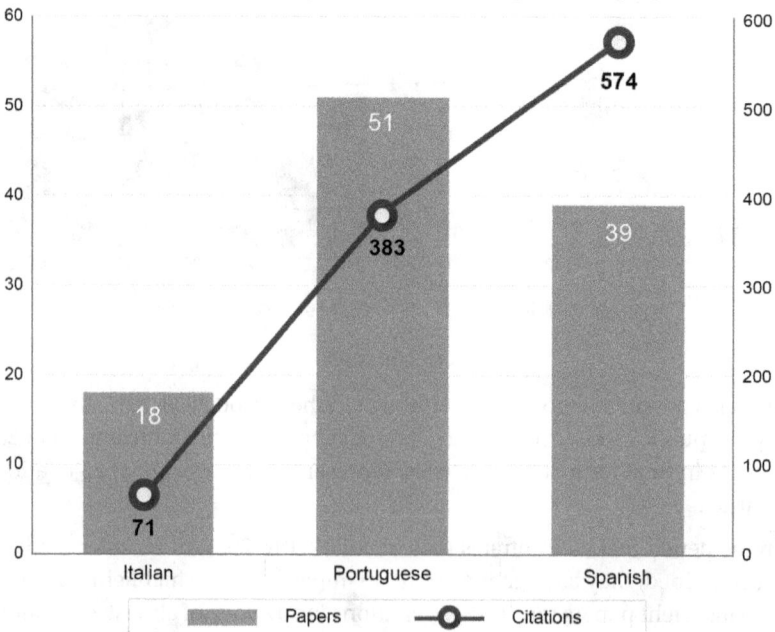

Source: the author.

An additional relevant analysis that can be made comprises the combined impact of publications according to the language (see Figure 3.4), where it is possible to notice that in absolute numbers, the 39 publications in Spanish have reached 574 citations in total (average of almost 15 citations per paper), followed by studies in Portuguese with 383 citations (average of almost eight citations per paper), and Italian studies with 71 citations (average of 4 citations per paper).

Thus, given these figures, it is fair to say that the publications in Spanish enjoy the highest level of impact in the sample, even being outnumbered by studies published in Portuguese (51 *vs* 39). Regarding the studies published in Italian, their reduced level of impact might probably be due to restricted dissemination compared to other languages.

# Chapter 4

# Analysis of studies published in Portuguese

*"In our work and in our living, we must recognise that difference is a reason for celebration and growth, rather than a reason for destruction".*

(Audre Lorde)

## Introduction

The present chapter starts with a brief overview of social media platforms in Brazil and Portugal with the aim of revealing some key data regarding their ubiquitous presence and popularity in both countries.

That being said, in the development of this chapter, the goal was to unveil the predominant themes investigated in the sample of studies and then, subsequently, analyse them. To this end, following the methodological approach suggested by Jorgensen and Phillips (2002), the papers were examined in an iterative process of interrogation to allow the emergence of key themes. As a consequence, it was possible to identify five main themes as follows: 1) the intersection of gender, race and class, 2) politically motivated hate speech, 3) homophobic hate speech, 4) social representation and xenophobic discourses, and 5) other social issues, what means varied themes that did not fit in other categories.

It is also recognised that the small sample of studies published in Portugal (just 3 in comparison to 48 in Brazil) represents an unintentional limitation because this reduced amount does not allow the development of a broader view of the prevailing types of online harassment and abuse in Portugal. Nonetheless, despite this limitation, it is understood that it does not jeopardise the objectives of the present study, and to address this issue, it has been chosen to develop a separate section to discuss the studies published in that country.

The chapter finishes with a small section that brings an overview of the social media platforms that have been examined the most in the studies published in Portuguese.

## Overview of social media landscape in Brazil and Portugal

Before starting to present and discuss the major findings regarding the sample of studies conducted in Brazil and Portugal, it is relevant to bring an overview of the presence of social media in both countries.

This approach aims to provide the reader with some contextual background in terms of the use of social media, the proportion of male and female users, and also which platforms are more popular in each country.

It is also true that the social media industry is extremely dynamic, and the figures portraying its performance are constantly evolving and subject to changes due to technological advancements, changes in users' behaviour, and national regulations. Thus, this overview should be seen more as a snapshot of a given moment in time rather than a definitive and immutable portrayal.

**Table 4.1**: Summary of social media data in Brazil and Portugal

| Countries and Metrics | | Brazil | Portugal |
|---|---|---|---|
| Country's Population (million) | | 215.8 | 10.26 |
| Active Social Media Users (million) | | 152.4 | 8.05 |
| Relative in Relation to the Population | | 70.6% | 78.5% |
| Daily Time Spent Using Social Media | | 3h 46min | 2h 25min |
| World Averagee | | 2h 31min | |
| Social Media Users | Male | 45.2% | 47.8% |
| | Female | 54.8% | 52.2% |
| Most Used Social Media Platforms | Facebook | 86.8% | 83.9% |
| | FB Messenger | 65.1% | 71.6% |
| | Instagram | 89.8% | 81.6% |
| | Telegram | 59% | 31% |
| | TikTok | 65.9% | 46% |
| | Twitter | 47.7% | 36.6% |
| | WhatsApp | 93.4% | 87.8% |

Source: The author based on Kemp (2023c; 2023a)

To this end, the major source of data comprises the yearly report developed by Kemp (2023c; 2023a) for three main reasons. First, because unlike several other reports produced by international consulting companies, the data are fully open access. Secondly, the author has been following this industry for many years, and the reports are consistent and homogenous over time. Finally, since the yearly reports cover a large number of countries, this allows the use of data all according to the same basis of comparison.

Along these lines and focusing the attention solely on the most relevant data in alignment with the scope of the present study, it is possible to notice some important aspects, as displayed in Table 4.1.

As the data reveals, WhatsApp, Facebook, and Instagram are by far the most used social media platforms in both countries, while others such as Twitter, TikTok, and Telegram are quite behind. Besides, since it is very common for people to have multiple accounts on different social media platforms, this explains why the accumulated relative values do not reach 100%.

Moreover, it also calls attention to the fact that female users in Brazil and Portugal outnumber male users. In the case of Brazil, the difference is considerably high (52.2% *vs* 45.2%), while in Portugal, although smaller, it is also expressive (52.2% *vs* 47.8%). Nonetheless, despite the higher proportion of female users of social media platforms, different studies have already revealed that male users are the ones most prone to be involved in cases of hate speech, which is also indicative of highly patriarchal societies where male figures feel empowered to display their dominance and masculinity (Erjavec and Kovačič, 2012; Trindade, 2018).

Then, two other aspects displayed in Table 4.1 are worth mentioning. First, the large relative proportion of social media users compared to the country's population, above 70%, what should be interpreted as a rate of the ubiquitous presence of social media platforms in peoples' lives. This figure indicates that the user base is so high that they symbolically, rather than literally, represent that share of the country's population.

Secondly, the daily average time people spend on social media comprises another distinctive aspect. In the case of Brazil, the average time is much higher than the global average of 2h 31 min, while in Portugal, it is slightly lower. Nevertheless, what is relevant to say concerning this particular metric is that the more time people remain connected to social media, the greater the chances of potentially being exposed to inappropriate content (e.g., hate speech, misogyny, racism, xenophobia, homophobia, etc.). Additionally, the greater the profit earned by the corporations, given that hateful content tends to generate high levels of engagement and longer exposition of pieces of advertisements (Aziz, 2020; BHRRC, 2020; Trindade, 2022).

Finally, another distinctive aspect to take into consideration is that although Facebook seems to be losing its leading position in the recent past regarding users' preferences, it still remains the world's largest social media platform in terms of active monthly users, with almost three billion people (Kemp, 2023h). Furthermore, the same Meta corporation owns WhatsApp, Facebook, Instagram, and FB Messenger[1].

Consequently, even if users migrate from one platform to another within this small group, by the end of the day, they are still engulfed in the same powerful and influential ecosystem that a single corporation owns.

## Main themes emerged from the sample of studies

### *The intersection of gender, race and class*

First, it calls attention to the fact that prominent female public figures are easily targeted by social media offenders. That is, they become victims of aggressive, misogynistic hate speech, as was the case with Brazil's former president Dilma Rousseff (Stocker and Dalmaso, 2016) and former city councillor Marielle Franco, who, even after being brutally assassinated in Rio de Janeiro in March 2018, still became a target of hate speech (Silveira-Barbosa and Rocha, 2018). Another prominent public figure that was the target of hate speech on Facebook comprised a Black female journalist (Rebs and Ernst, 2017), and similarly to what happened with Marielle Franco, it was possible to observe the intersectionality of gender and race fuelling the hateful discourses. In the case of the hateful manifestations against Dilma Rousseff, gender intersects with far-right political discourses.

Still, in the case of Dilma Rousseff, given her former position as head of state (i.e., a woman performing a leadership role), the authors Stocker and Dalmaso (2016) argue that the misogynistic hate speech depicted her as incapable of leading the country, and made extensive use of ridicule, irony, and sarcasm to disqualify her as a woman and as a political leader.

Furthermore, other prominent female public figures whom offenders in Brazilian social media have targeted comprise a group of eight senators who had expressed their disagreement with the ongoing impeachment process against President Dilma Rousseff (Silva and Sampaio, 2017). In this case, the discourses on Facebook were characterised by the extensive use of aggressive insults, stereotyping, blaming, manifestations of heteronormative white superiority, and animalisation of the female figure.

---

[1] Additionally, as previously addressed in Chapter 1, they have added Threads to their portfolio of platforms, which resembles 'X' (formerly known as Twitter).

In fact, evolving from the reflection raised in these four studies and establishing a dialogue with others in the sample, it is possible to notice that in strongly patriarchal societies, women performing prominent social roles might trigger a sense of discomfort in many men, which is expressed through misogynistic hate speech (Costa, 2017). Such reactions have the twofold goal to challenge women's social progress and symbolic achievements, reposition them in submissive conditions, or, when intersecting with race and ethnicity, also position them in racial and social inferiority conditions.

Additionally, while the offenders convey direct misogynistic hate speech on several occasions, as revealed in the studies mentioned earlier, they are indirectly manifested in other instances. This dynamic is observed through the over-valorisation of masculinity in opposition to feminism and feminists, as seen in the studies conducted by Martins (2019) and Anjos (2022), through the reinforcement of heteronormative values to challenge gender ideology (Pereira, 2017; Henn *et al.*, 2019; Storto and Zanardi, 2019), and the naturalisation of sexist values (Peres-Neto and Pereira, 2019).

Indeed, the dichotomy of *us vs them* seems to be at the core of such discourses, as revealed by Storto and Zanardi (2019). The authors explain that supporters of this dualistic worldview claim normative values for themselves (e.g., evangelical people, honest, Christians, liberals, conservative) while assigning negative attributes to 'the others' (e.g., communists, non-Christians, socialists, evil people, and so forth).

Nonetheless, although several studies reveal that social media platforms have become a breeding ground for the manifestation of a myriad of racist discourses against Black people, it is also a space for resistance and social activism (e.g., Borges and Melo, 2019; Feitosa e Paiva and Silva, 2019; Fernandes *et al.*, 2020).

Supporting evidence for this claim is found, for example, in the study conducted by Flannery (2017), where the author investigates the construction of networks of solidarity on Facebook to provide moral support to victims of racist discourses in the online environment.

In a subsequent study, Lopes and Figueiredo (2018) explain how groups of Black Brazilian women have organised in Facebook communities to foster antiracist education and Black empowerment. The distinctive aspect behind this initiative is that their empowerment discourses aim to highlight both blackness and natural Afro hairstyle because darker skin tone and Black hair comprise features often negatively explored in racist discourses.

Furthermore, the study conducted by Silva (2020a) brings to the surface the relevance of organised Black feminist groups in occupying virtual spaces to the use of digital technology as a tool of resistance and a powerful vehicle for antiracist education and political positioning.

Finally, another important factor weaving together these last three studies (Flannery, 2017; Lopes and Figueiredo, 2018; Silva, 2020a) comprises the fact that Black women are at the forefront of the antiracist cyber activism in Brazil, and despite being one of the most frequent victims, they are leading the way to challenge Brazil's ingrained and enduring racist ideologies (Trindade, 2020a).

### *Politically motivated hate speech*

Prominent public figures such as artists, professional sports people, journalists, social media influencers, politicians, and members of government have a big responsibility beyond their institutional or professional roles. Since they tend to enjoy high visibility and often have great access to various means of mass communication, anything they say can reach a wide audience and influence many other people's way of thinking, points of view and behaviour.

Within this line of reasoning, it is possible to observe that Maia and Rezende (2015) reveal that a racist statement delivered by a Brazilian parliamentarian during a TV interview has triggered dozens of supporting discourses on YouTube, Facebook and blogs. The white male parliamentarian was questioned in March 2011 about how he would react if one of his sons fell in love with a Black woman. In response, he said they would not incur such a 'risk' because his sons had been 'well-educated' and were not 'promiscuous'.

Among the supporting discourses published on social media calls attention one that says: 'In my church, Blacks, homeless people, gays, lesbians, atheists, dwarfs, and mentally ill people will not inherit the heavenly kingdom. At the same time, I am happy for being white because the Lord has already chosen me'. Thus, this sample of social media comment represents a strong illustrative example of the negative influence triggered by controversial discourses delivered by prominent public figures, as previously explained.

Moreover, the study conducted by Maia and Rezende (2015) brings two additional contributions. First, as commonly observed nowadays, it reveals how discourses posted in a given communication channel can easily circulate across several others, amplifying their reach, reverberation, and impact. Secondly, it contributes to the debate regarding the interplay between hate speech and politics.

This finding is corroborated by two subsequent studies conducted by Wainberg and Müller (2017) and Carvalho *et al.* (2018) regarding the proliferation of hate speech on social media during the 2014 Brazilian presential elections and their potential to attract and influence voters' opinions.

What is also important to observe is the fact that, according to several studies, often politically motivated hate speech on social media is permeated not only by political ideologies (e.g., conservative *vs* progressive policies) but also by a myriad of discriminatory discourses. Amidst it, Silva and Botelho-Francisco (2020) have examined 3,550 comments on the Facebook pages of three far-right Brazilian parliamentarians. These politicians are notorious for delivering public discourses expressing religious intolerance (especially against faiths of African origin), racism, sexism, and homophobia. Consequently, the authors have identified that the politicians' supporters express equivalent levels of hate and intolerance on social media.

On top of that, what is highly problematic is that politically motivated hate speech can depict political opponents as enemies rather than adversaries simply advocating different arguments. In this context, Silva *et al.* (2021) have examined 3.8 million Facebook comments and discovered that dualistic political hate speech (i.e., conveying ideas such as *us vs them*) is the most prevalent, followed by LGBTQ+ phobia and xenophobia. Indeed, this finding dialogues with the argument raised by Storto and Zanardi (2019) in the sense that supporters of hate speech tend to claim normative values to themselves and deviant attributes to 'the others'.

Furthermore, it is also very interesting to understand how this duality of *us vs them* can operate because sometimes it might not be very clear. On this aspect, Maynard (2014) makes an important contribution with a cross-cultural study examining Argentinian and Brazilian fascist virtual communities. The author explains that while in Argentina, the 'others' are clearly the Jews, in Brazil, there is not a single 'Jew' but many. That is, "it can be Black, gay, homosexual, communist, women, and also Jew" (Maynard, 2014, p. 78). In other words, based on this explanation, the politically motivated discriminatory discourses on social media are supported not only by ideologies of white supremacy but also by contrasting conservative behavioural ideals.

In complement to this reflection, Silva et al. (2022) raise an important argumentation regarding the naturalisation of 'dischargeable' lives, which comprises the idea that certain 'others' (frequently comprised of young Black male individuals, lower class, and *favela* residents) are worthless and, consequently, the impact of the violent loss of their lives is downplayed. It is assumed and implied that, since these individuals live in that environment of social deprivation, they might also be 'involved' with illegal activities such as drug trafficking and then, their assassination is a motive of no surprise.

Nevertheless, continues Silva *et al.* (2022), this myopic approach conveniently disregards the condition of vulnerability of the victim. It supports the depiction of 'the other' as an enemy to be defeated by all means and the legitimisation of necropolitics ideals.

Finally, what cannot be taken out of the equation in the case of hate speech on social media is that it can lead towards acts of violence and physical aggression in the offline context, which is very problematic. Therefore, as previously explained, prominent public figures should be highly vigilant regarding what they say and post on social media because the impact and reverberation of their discourses can potentially go well beyond political rhetoric.

### Homophobic hate speech

According to the most recent edition of a yearly report addressing violence against transsexual people, Brazil occupies the top position for the 14th consecutive year as the country with the highest rate of assassinations (Benevides, 2023; Lucca, 2023). This finding also aligns with data published by the organisation Transgender Europe, which reveals 1,741 assassinations in Brazil between 2008 and September 2022. For the sake of proportion, in the same period, the second position is occupied by Mexico with 649 assassinations, followed by the US in third place with 375 assassinations, Colombia (233), Venezuela (131), and finally Argentina in fifth place with 113 assassinations (TGEU, 2023).

The importance of highlighting these particular figures lays in the fact that sexual orientation and LGBTQ+ phobia comprise another predominant social issue explored in several studies, and the number just displayed contributes to providing an overview of the seriousness of the subject matter.

Within it, is possible to notice that Bastos *et al.* (2017, p. 14) raise a relevant point explaining that "homophobia can be observed in jokes, physical and verbal aggressions experienced in diverse daily circumstances and including rejection within one's own family". Moreover, this type of discriminatory attitude places 'the other' as a stranger and an anomaly.

Nevertheless, taking into consideration an awareness campaign against homophobia fostered on Facebook by Brazil's Secretary of Human Rights, the authors have a positive view of the potential of social media. In other words, they see cyberspace not only as an environment to disseminate hate but also as a space of resistance and construction of meanings (Bastos *et al.*, 2017). In a certain way, this reflection dialogues with the studies conducted by Lopes and Figueiredo (2018) and Silva (2020a), as previously addressed in the section *The Intersection of Gender, Race and Class.*

In continuation, it is possible to observe that certain social groups adopt a sort of indirect approach to convey homophobic ideals. In this regard, Alves and Paulo (2017) have analysed a series of posts and comments published in a

Facebook community fostering their pride in being straight[2] men. The idea advocated by the administrators and supporters is to confront the different values, compare masculinity and highlight their heteronormative role.

Furthermore, Silva (2018) develops a similar investigation and discusses the inherent problems with social media discourses fostering compulsory heterosexuality ideals. In other words, these studies reveal that this type of homophobic discourse on social media (i.e., highlighting heteronormative values) is centred on behaviour, especially because many of them confront 'normal' masculinity with 'deviant' homosexuality.

Indeed, analysing other studies in the sample (Silva and Aléssio, 2019; Silva *et al.*, 2020; Silva and Silva, 2021), it is possible to observe that they share a common feature. Homophobic hate speech on social media is frequently permeated with a variety of conflicting and contrasting values orbiting around the duality 'normal' *vs* 'deviant', which represents an umbrella for a multitude of simplistic ambivalent comparisons (e.g., right *vs* wrong, sacred *vs* pagan, ethical *vs* unethical, moral *vs* immoral, and so forth) and never giving room for divergent standpoints and diversified world views.

### Social representation and xenophobic discourses

According to authors such as Wagner (1994), Moscovici (1988; 1994), and Fernandes (2003), social representations result from the individuality of the members of a given social group; their interaction with this collectivity and is manifested through the linguistic signs used by them. Moreover, the representations of reality are constructed by individuals to interpret, understand, and create their social identities. Then, following this line of reflection, it is possible to observe that the interaction between the individual and society make them, in the first moment, position themselves in certain social groups through their identity.

Besides, the relationship between observer and observed is impregnated with estrangement, and both parties resort to meaning mechanisms that allow them to process and translate reality mentally. Amidst it, this estrangement represents a difficulty experienced by the observer in assigning meaning to the observed (i.e., an individual, a social group, or a fact of life) and accepting their inherent differences (Oliva, 2003).

---

[2] Although 'straight' is understood as the synonym of heterosexual, it might eventually be a problematic terminology because it also means right, direct, righteous, honest, correct, erect, upright. Thus, whoever is not 'straight' might be the opposite of this array of meanings. Consequently, although it has been employed here, it is considered relevant to add this brief reflexivity argumentation.

Thus, bearing in mind that social representations involve a process of interpreting reality and the consequent positioning of the individual before it, its instrumentalization occurs through what is called 'social knowledge' (Fernandes, 2003). In other words, 'social knowledge' encompasses a set of ideologies, values, and beliefs that allow the observer to assess and interpret reality.

Thus, having introduced this brief conceptual explanation, it is possible to observe that a few studies in the sample have examined the issue of social representation on social media. In the first place, in the study conducted by Vitali *et al.* (2019), the authors explore how the lack of public knowledge regarding the difference between assigned sex at birth, sexual orientation, and gender identity can contribute to the construction of distorted and inaccurate social representations of transsexuality in the online environment.

In another study, Luz (2019) examines the collective social representation of blackness in Brazilian politics. Bearing in mind that ingrained racist ideologies assign certain limited and often disqualified social roles for Black Brazilians, the authors investigated how these elements interact to build the social representation of a prominent Black male political figure. In other words, in this context, the social representation is permeated with estrangement since, in the mind of social media users, that particular Black figure is performing a social role usually associated exclusively with whiteness rather than blackness.

Then, intertwined with this reflection, Silva (2020b) raises an important debate concerning the role played by deep-rooted racist bias embedded in the development of algorithms of modern digital technologies such as search engines, social media platforms and face recognition software, influencing their depiction of non-white people. The author argues that the social representation portrayed by these technologies reflects, replicates and reinforces society's negative perceptions of non-white people.

Evolving from the reflection addressed in these social representation studies, it is also possible to notice a certain degree of relationship between them and other works investigating xenophobic discourses on social media. Amidst it, Seara and Cabral (2020) explore aggressive anti-immigrant discourses in Portugal and Brazil. The authors argue that the analysed social media comments revealed the continuous call for expelling immigrants from both countries. Moreover, the discourses convey a series of negative depictions of immigrants, disqualify them, and blame them either as the single source or the key worsening factor of social problems.

Additionally, Moura and Souza (2019) have conducted another study examining xenophobic discourses on social media in Brazil targeted at Venezuelan immigrants. In alignment with the previous study, it can be observed that the authors have also identified that the social media discourses negatively portray immigrants and blame them as the cause of a series of social problems (e.g., increasing criminality, prostitution, poverty, etc.). Furthermore, the authors reveal that social media users tend to employ possessive pronouns (e.g., my country, my land, my right, we are in charge, etc.) to express their anti-immigrant sentiment and as a linguistic mechanism to challenge the 'invaders'.

Nonetheless, xenophobic discourses are quite problematic because many people fail to acknowledge the fact that immigration is often a challenging circumstance for people who move to an alien country. The reason is that immigration is experienced as a downgrading of their fundamental rights with severe emotional, economic, and legal difficulties involved when settling in a new society. On top of that, according to the European Commission against Racism and Intolerance, people exposed to discrimination and intolerance often have neither the capacity nor the resources to enforce their rights (ECRI, 2019; 2020).

### Other social issues

While in the previous sections, it was possible to group a selection of convergent studies addressing similar subject matters, the sample of papers in Portuguese also brings other works exploring a variety of topics that not necessarily fit in the previous thematic sections.

Having explained that, a distinctive characteristic of this group of studies comprises the fact that some authors have examined the phenomenon of hate speech on social media (Hilgert and Neto, 2017; Mercuri and Lima-Lopes, 2020; Quadrado and Ferreira, 2020). However, different from other authors previously analysed that have focused their attention on specific types of hate speech (e.g., racist, homophobic, misogynist, xenophobic, etc.), the authors aforementioned have approached the issue more broadly.

In this context, it is possible to observe that, starting from the specific event of the killing of 60 rebellious prisoners in Manaus penitentiary in January 2017, Hilgert and Neto (2017) have examined 427 comments on Facebook to analyse what type of discourses had been triggered by this event. Their investigation revealed the predominance of hate speech endorsing the killings and an echo chamber effect where like-minded people express uniform agreement among themselves and vehemently repel dissonant voices. Indeed, it also becomes clear that this reflection dialogues directly with the analysis of echo chamber effect developed in Chapter 2.

In the case of the study conducted by Mercuri and Lima-Lopes (2020), the authors have analysed political discussions on Twitter triggered by a general strike scheduled to take place on 28 April 2017 aimed at protesting against labour and pension reforms. Since many people opposed joining the general strike, the authors identified that a few social media influencers played a considerable role in disseminating hate speech on Twitter, which was widely and instantaneous spread. In a certain way, this study dialogues with the work conducted by Di Fátima *et al.* (2020) in Portugal in the sense that both studies demonstrate the significant weight played by a handful of influencers in disseminating disinformation, bigotry, and also discriminatory ideologies and turning them 'viral'.

Regarding Quadrado and Ferreira (2020), the authors have developed bibliographical research to support a critical analysis questioning the extension of which hate and intolerance on social media might constitute a risk in the face of the democratic rule of law. Their evaluation concluded that these modern digital technologies contribute to the emergence of profiles marked by intolerance and extremist discriminatory ideologies. Secondly, this overall picture poses serious threats to democracy in many societies.

Another topic that many authors have not explored in the sample of studies comprises the phenomenon of cyberbullying in the school context. Within it, based on previous studies, Azevedo *et al.* (2012) present a theoretical analysis addressing bullying and cyberbullying in school and their relationship with the psychic structures of the subjects involved in such practices. The authors advocate that the increasingly ubiquitous presence of digital technologies such as social media in people's lives poses challenging impacts on various aspects of social life. Among them, the wide and instantaneous dissemination of virtual violence can be highlighted, which ultimately also brings irreparable damage to the psychism and the social lives of cyberbullying victims.

In continuation with the analysis of the studies, it is possible to observe that Petry and Nascimento (2016) have developed a work examining people's opinions published on Facebook regarding the controversial topic of reduction of the legal age for criminal charges. The analysis of dozens of users' comments revealed that the individuals subject to the change in regulation are predominantly lower-class Black teenagers, whose citizenship rights are being ignored and labelled in disqualifying categories such as 'monsters', 'underage thugs', and 'inhuman'. Moreover, the authors continue, users' comments on social media rely on ideologies that depict Black adolescents as 'problematic' and needing corrective measures, which should be tough and merciless.

Indeed, paying close attention to the discursive strategy employed by many social media users, such as in the study conducted by Petry and Nascimento (2016), Mercuri and Lima-Lopes (2020), it is possible to notice that excesses and exaggerations characterise them. In this regard, Rebs (2017) has analysed dozens of Facebook comments belittling a prominent Black female actress and identified elements such as the employment of degrading vocabulary, reinforcement of discriminatory ideologies and demonstration of gender and racial superiority.

Within it, Rebs (2017) explains that the embedded meaning and the strength of hateful discourses fostered on social media go beyond the victims' public humiliation and mere offence. The users are seeking the affirmation of an ideology that is contextualised by a historical subject, who acts under the effect of the unconscious, building a reality of violence that is justified by their aim to disqualify and belittle 'the other'. Thus, the excesses present in their discursive strategies also afford the users a high level of visibility, popularity among like-minded people, 'authority' and 'reputation' in the online environment. In other words, they can become influencers and set the trend according to their discriminatory and hateful ideologies.

Finally, despite all the criticism raised by numerous authors regarding the role played by social media platforms in disseminating hate speech, Silva *et al.* (2019) present a very different perspective. The authors have developed an innovative comparative assessment of Facebook, Twitter, and YouTube in order to understand their respective approaches to tackling cyberhate. To this end, they have analysed the corporations' policies and community terms within the timeframe 2015-2018, and the fulfilment of their commitments agreed with the Anti-Defamation League in 2013[3]. Overall, it is possible to observe that Silva *et al.* (2019) have concluded that the results of their investigation suggest that, among the three platforms, Facebook had invested the most in strategies to combat intolerance and incivility online. Nonetheless, the authors admit that there was a lack of clarity concerning how the corporation is doing what they are saying they are doing. Ultimately, the authors argue that the three platforms showed considerable improvements in operational structure to report cyberhate. However, they were still inefficient in content moderation, removal, and containment of cyberhate propagation.

## A glimpse of social media in Portugal

As previously explained, a limitation of the present study comprises the fact that the search for open-access studies published in Portuguese brought considerably fewer papers addressing Portugal than Brazil. However, although this section does not have the ambition to portray a comprehensive picture of the varying types of online harassment and abuse in Portugal, even so, it was considered relevant to group them in a single section rather than leaving them dispersed among many others.

---

[3] The Anti-Defamation League is a Jewish non-governmental organization based in the United States specializing in civil rights law (https://www.adl.org/).

In this way, the first aspect that calls attention comprises an innovative study conducted by Di Fátima *et al.* (2020) examining the interplay between social media influencers and football. Their study has revealed the significant weight played by a handful of influencers in directing and setting the trends of discussion in a given topic (in this particular case, a football match, Porto *vs* Benfica). Moreover, their study also revealed that the reach of comments went well beyond Portugal and reached users based in several other countries, which reinforces the understanding that discourses fostered on social media are not constrained by geographical borders.

In another study, Costa (2020) investigates the phenomenon of hate speech on Facebook, particularly the triggering elements of hateful discourses. The study revealed a strong correlation between a set of themes such as crime/ aggression, football, politics, religion, and wrongdoing with the enactment of hate speech. Furthermore, it was also possible to identify a sort of snowball effect, where the posts with the highest amount of insults tend to create greater engagement among users (e.g., share, like, and dislike) and consequently an increasing number of comments.

Finally, the study conducted by Teles (2020) brings to the surface the issue of discriminatory discourses on Twitter endorsing and naturalising police brutality against the Black community in Portugal. The author has identified that, overall, users' discourses conveyed a series of ingrained racist perceptions concerning Afro-descendant individuals in Portuguese society, often placing them in a condition of social inferiority. Additionally, Teles (2020) complements arguing that social media platforms like Twitter are used as a medium to express narratives that not only reinforce a myriad of discriminatory stereotypes but also endorse and naturalise brutal police action against 'the others'.

To sum up, it can be said that, in a certain way, the arguments raised by these three authors (Costa, 2020; Di Fátima *et al.*, 2020; Teles, 2020) coalesce with the work developed by Seara and Cabral (2020) who have examined xenophobic discourses on social media in Portugal and Brazil, as previously discussed. In both circumstances, hate speech is employed as a discursive strategy to challenge and disqualify the undesirable 'other' (i.e., Black immigrants).

### Overview of the social media platforms most examined

The first section of the present chapter presented an overview of the most relevant data regarding social media in Brazil and Portugal, revealing that the three most popular platforms in both countries are Facebook, Instagram, and WhatsApp. Thus, it is not surprising to discover that also the majority of the studies have examined varying types of online harassment and abuse manifested on Facebook, followed by Twitter, YouTube, and Instagram (see Figure 4.1).

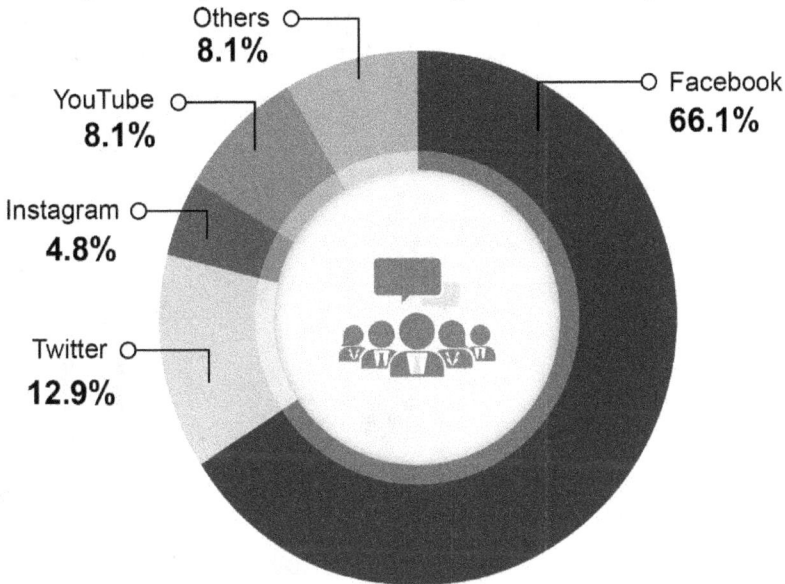

**Figure 4.1**: Proportion of studies according to the social media platform

Source: the author

A possible explanatory hypothesis for this strong predominance is due first to Facebook's high popularity, as the data in Table 4.1 clearly demonstrates. Secondly, because, as argued by Bliuc *et al.* (2018), Trindade (2020b), Matamoros-Fernandez and Farkas (2021), alongside several other authors, Facebook has become a breeding ground for the manifestation of a wide variety of hate speech and bigotry. Finally, there is an understanding that, compared to other social media platforms, researchers might consider it more feasible to collect publicly available textual data from Facebook than other platforms, especially for the development of qualitative analysis, which is the case in most of the studies in the sample.

In complement to that, it is also possible to notice that influential studies, such as Wilson *et al.* (2012) and Caers *et al.* (2013), have also chosen Facebook as a study objects. Furthermore, as advocated by Caers *et al.* (2013), taking into account that this social media platform has become the largest one in its category and the most influential, it has set the industry's trends and technological standards. Consequently, it is understandable that it has also become the most examined.

On the other hand, this large predominance of studies exploring mostly Facebook and Twitter also means that there is a considerable gap in the literature and big publication potential for studies exploring Instagram, TikTok, Telegram, YouTube, and WhatsApp.

Therefore, although the sample of studies in Portuguese has revealed this snapshot where Facebook and Twitter appear in the foreground, it cannot be disregarded that there are still plenty of underexplored possibilities in the background.

# Chapter 5

# Analysis of studies published in Spanish

*"We are human beings like everyone else, with
different political and ideological views. In my case,
for example, between left-wing and right-wing, I am
still a Black woman".*

(Sueli Carneiro)

## Introduction

Similar to the approach adopted in Chapter 4, the present chapter starts with a brief overview of key data regarding social media presence in Spanish-speaking countries represented in the sample of studies.

Subsequently, the chapter aims to unveil the prevailing themes addressed in the sample of 39 papers and analyse them. To this end, the papers were also examined in an iterative process of interrogation, as suggested by Jorgensen and Phillips (2002), which led to the identification of three main themes: 1) xenophobic discourses, 2) politically motivated hate speech, and 3) deep-rooted and enduring racism.

There is also an additional section that combines a small group of different studies whose themes did not fit in any of the main categories. The chapter finishes then with a brief section dedicated to developing some comments regarding the prevailing social media platforms examined in the studies in Spanish.

## Overview of social media landscape in Spanish-speaking countries

To start with, it is important to explain that there is a lack of complete information regarding half of the countries represented in the sample, and consequently, it is not possible to have a more comprehensive picture as developed in Chapter 4. This unintentional limitation is beyond the author's control, and it is due to the actual lack of data in the respective countries report.

**Table 5.1**: Summary of social media data in Spanish-speaking countries

| Countries and Metrics | | Argentina | Colombia | Costa Rica | El Salvador | Equador | Mexico | Peru | Spain |
|---|---|---|---|---|---|---|---|---|---|
| Country's Population (million) | | 45.63 | 51.96 | 5.19 | 6.35 | 18.1 | 128 | 34.19 | 47.54 |
| Active Social Media Users (million) | | 36.35 | 38.45 | 3.83 | 4.0 | 13.3 | 94 | 25.05 | 40.7 |
| Relative in Relation to the Population | | 84.4% | 74% | 73.7% | 63% | 73.5% | 73.4% | 73.3% | 85.6% |
| Daily Time Spent Using Social Media | | 3h 15min | 3h 32min | - | - | - | 3h 21min | - | 1h 55min |
| World Averagee | | 2h 31min | | | | | | | |
| Social Media Users | Male | 47.9% | 48.3% | 48.7% | 48.1% | 50% | 47.3% | 51.8% | 48.9% |
| | Female | 52.1% | 51.7% | 51.3% | 51.9% | 50% | 52.7% | 48.2% | 51.1% |
| Most Used Social Media Platforms | Facebook | 84% | 90.5% | - | - | - | 92.9% | - | 72.5% |
| | FB Messenger | 56.8% | 72.2% | - | - | - | 80.3% | - | 38.1% |
| | Instagram | 86% | 85.6% | - | - | - | 79.4% | - | 74.9% |
| | Telegram | 39.8% | 51.9% | - | - | - | 44.5% | - | 41.3% |
| | TikTok | 53.6% | 67.9% | - | - | - | 73.6% | - | 47.3% |
| | Twitter | 49% | 52.4% | - | - | - | 53.7% | - | 47.7% |
| | WhatsApp | 93.1% | 92.4% | - | - | - | 92.9% | - | 89.7% |

Source: The author based on Kemp (2023f; 2023e; 2023g; 2023d; 2023k; 2023j; 2023l; 2023b)

However, despite this limitation, the available data allows the identification first that apart from Ecuador and Peru, female users outnumber male users in the remaining six countries. The smallest relative difference is observed in Spain (51.1% female *vs* 48.9% male), and the highest difference is in Argentina (52.1% female *vs* 47.9% male). Yet, these figures are smaller than those observed in Brazil and Portugal, as discussed in Chapter 4.

Moreover, quite similar to what is observed in Brazil and Portugal, the proportion of social media users compared to the country's population is also high. Except for El Salvador, with just 63%, all the other countries show rates above 70%, and Spain holds the highest rate (85.6%).

Regarding the daily average time people spend connected to social media, the available data from four countries show that Spanish users spent much less than the global average (just 1h 55 min *vs* 2h 31 min), while in Argentina, Colombia, and Mexico, users spend more than 3h. So, this level of usage is equivalent to that observed in Brazil and well above the global average.

Regarding the most used social media platforms, although in four countries there is no available data, it is possible to infer that, at least what concerns the order of preference, there might not be a substantial difference. Thus, based on the figures presented by Argentina, Colombia, Mexico, and Spain, it becomes clear that the corporation Meta dominates the social media industry across the eight Spanish-speaking countries, taking into account that all their four platforms (Facebook, FB Messenger, Instagram, and WhatsApp) are always among the top three most popular.

Other platforms such as TikTok, Telegram, and Twitter also enjoy a considerable share of users' preferences, but ultimately, the data suggests that Meta is currently a very successful business enterprise that manages to retain the largest proportion of social media users engulfed in their powerful ecosystem.

## Main themes emerged from the sample of studies

### *Xenophobic discourses*

The mass movement of people around the world is an ancient phenomenon, and there are many factors contributing to migration, such as, for example, a) economic, b) demographic, c) socio-cultural, d) political, e) wars and armed conflicts, and f) drastic or severe changes in climatic conditions.

Amidst it, recent data reveals that the world is experiencing the biggest displacement of people since World War II, with more than 22 million displaced from their home countries (WEF, 2016).

Yet, according to Torkington and Ribeiro (2019), there have been increasing debates in academia regarding the 'correct' labelling of different forms of migration. This subject matter is of high relevance because "the discursive construction of people 'on the move' may lead not only to the formation of stereotypical social representations but also, ultimately, to different treatment of different groups of people in 'host' countries" (Torkington and Ribeiro, 2019, p. 22).

Along these lines, it is possible to observe that xenophobia comprises a prominent social issue explored in studies published in Spanish. In this context, Reyes Vázquez and Barrios de la O (2019) conducted a sentiment analysis on 1,063 tweets (461 in Spanish and 602 in English) published in March 2019. The tweets addressed the subject matter of a caravan of Central American immigrants arriving in the south of Mexico, however, with the US as their final desired destination.

The analysis revealed that the discourses published on Twitter displayed aspects of racism and xenophobia against immigrants in such a way that some of the most frequent words employed by users encompass 'invasion' and 'delinquency'. In complement to this study, it is possible to notice that Pérez Díaz and Aguilar Pérez (2021) have also examined the same subject matter of the caravan of immigrants, however, analysing the intersection among negative social representation, racism, and discrimination. To this end, the authors have conducted a content analysis on comments posted on Facebook and Twitter regarding a piece of news addressing an immigrant caravan arriving in Mexico in November 2018.

The key aspect of this study comprises the fact that in many situations, xenophobic narratives explore the characteristics of a single individual as a representative of a whole social group. In other words, since certain negative stigmas and stereotypes might be attributed to ethnic minorities by hegemonic groups, social media users expand them to the entire population of immigrants from 'undesirable' or second-class countries.

In another content analysis study conducted by Olmos Alcaraz (2018), the author has also examined xenophobic discourses published by Facebook users, and the author has identified that racism is often a correlated component of these manifestations, which coalesces with the findings revealed by Pérez Díaz and Aguilar Pérez (2021).

Overall, what can be observed is that the xenophobic comments published on Facebook reveal four main embedded themes: 1) securing the country's boundaries, 2) threshold of intolerance, 3) blaming immigration as the source of social issues and competing for limited resources, and 4) the immigrant depicted as the enemy (Olmos Alcaraz, 2018).

Indeed, the analysis of xenophobic discourses on social media reveals that different studies conducted in diverse social contexts share a relatively high degree of convergence. It means that not only Olmos Alcaraz (2018) and Pérez Díaz and Aguilar Pérez (2021) have found the intersection of racism, stereotyping and negative social representation in xenophobic discourses. Also, Fernández Fernández *et al.* (2020) have identified the same aspects.

These authors have conducted a sentiment analysis on almost two million Twitter posts published between June and October 2018 addressing the arrival of immigrants aboard a boat in Spain. The study suggests that the absence of factual and accurate information regarding immigrants has led to irrational, rushed and emotive judgement of the immigrants by many social media users, which contributed to the reinforcement of a series of negative stereotypes about them (Fernández Fernández *et al.*, 2020).

Furthermore, as explained by Torkington and Ribeiro (2019), often, negative depictions of immigrants portray them as 'intruders'. As a consequence, in the collective mindset, they play the role of being prone to be involved in illicit activities, they are considered the source of several social problems, they compete for limited resources, and they trigger the moral 'duty' to protect the country's borders against such 'invasion'.

Another important aspect to highlight comprises the fact that most of the time, the mainstream international media tends to give more emphasis to conflicting and controversial cases of immigration involving people arriving in European countries and in the US, as also reflected in several studies (e.g., Oehmichen, 2018; Valdez-Apolo *et al.*, 2019; Marta-Lazo *et al.*, 2020; Teso Craviotto and Acevedo, 2022). However, as previously mentioned, the phenomenon of immigration is not only ancient but also global.

Within it, it is possible to notice that Altamirano and Torres-Toukoumidis (2021) have examined 780 xenophobic comments against Venezuelan immigrants in Ecuador. The comments were published between April 2018 and January 2019 on the Facebook page of two major Ecuadorian newspapers (*El Mercurio* and *El Tiempo*). Although the results do not overlap with conceptual findings of other studies, they reveal some worrisome figures: a) 60.7% of the sample of comments disqualify Venezuelans due to their enduring and challenging political, cultural, social situation, and economic b) 50% of the comments demands expelling the Venezuelans from Ecuador, c) 46.4% of the comments blame the Venezuelans as the source of social problems in Ecuador, and d) just 21.8% of the comments are supportive to the Venezuelan population.

Additionally, Venezuelans have also been the victims of xenophobic discourses on Facebook and Twitter in Peru, as revealed in the study conducted by Vega (2022) analysed. In this case, the triggering event comprised the access to COVID-19 vaccination, where many Peruvian social media users unleashed xenophobic sentiments against the immigrants. As previously addressed in this section, usually, this sort of discourse is fuelled by distorted perceptions depicting immigrants as 'invaders' and competing for limited resources such as, in this case, access to the public health system.

Evolving from this analysis, in Costa Rica, social media users have expressed a series of xenophobic manifestations against a new regulation issued by educational authorities establishing that on 30 September 2016, primary schools should play Nicaragua's national anthem in celebration of the patriotic month. The regulation had been put forward to be effective just in a selection of schools with a high proportion of Nicaraguan students. Nonetheless, not only the regulation was met with disappointment and scepticism but also with aggressive, xenophobic discourses and sexism against the female educational minister.

The study conducted by Solano Rivera and Ramírez Caro (2019) revealed the construction and dissemination of stereotypes portraying Nicaraguans as violent, delinquent, prone to be involved with illicit activities, useless, dangerous and threatening. As for the sexist comments, they disqualify the female minister and challenge her political competence for the role, which coalesces with the findings revealed by Stocker and Dalmaso (2016) regarding Brazilian female politicians, as previously discussed in Chapter 4.

Ultimately, analysing these studies, it becomes clear first that, as Torkington and Ribeiro (2019) argued, discursive strategies employed by dominant groups set the tone regarding how different social groups are received or repelled in 'host' countries. Amidst it, Valdez-Apolo et al. (2019) reinforce this argumentation, explaining that on social media, while immigrants are predominantly depicted in negative 'colours', the same does not happen with refugees, who usually enjoy better reception and greater integration opportunities.

Secondly, in this overall context, the Group Conflict Theory states that ethnic prejudice and anti-immigrant feelings comprise defence mechanisms employed by hegemonic social groups to safeguard their established positions and protect resources that they perceive to be threatened by the arrival of immigrants (e.g., jobs, social benefits, healthcare, access to public education, etc.). Finally, the Social Identity Theory explains that external groups of individuals (i.e., immigrants) perceived as threatening a nation's distinctive identity are likely to trigger hostility (D'Ancona, 2018).

### *Politically motivated hate speech*

Since Barack Obama's successful 2008 election, the interplay between social media and political discourses has become increasingly strong and more common (Cogburn and Espinoza-Vasquez, 2011). In fact, after that, the world has witnessed a significant surge of far-right political figures such as Donald Trump in the US, Jair Bolsonaro in Brazil, and Mateo Salvini in Italy, who, besides sharing extremist nationalist views, are also avid social media users (Trindade, 2020c). Additionally, on several occasions, Mauricio Macri (Argentina), Donald Trump (US), Jair Bolsonaro (London), and Iván Duque (Colombia) have openly disseminated discourses conveying racist, sexist, xenophobic, and homophobic ideologies (Solano Rivera and Ramírez Caro, 2019). Thus, this brief account contributes to providing an overview of the current scenario regarding political discourses on social media.

Within this context, users are also influenced by such discourses circulating online, where social media becomes a stage where ideological disputes occur and the polarisation between different political stances emerge.

In Peru, for example, Cerna Aragón (2017) explains that during the 2016 presidential campaign, several social media users, coined as *Fujitrolls*, have been accused of being paid by Keiko Fujimori's political party for creating fake Twitter accounts to aggressively attack rival candidates.

Indeed, this scenario leads to the reflection that social media has contributed to a challenging and somewhat blurred scenario where the truth can be manipulated according to certain political agendas or convenience, what became known as 'post-truth', as explained by Hernández-Santaolalla and Sola-Morales (2019). Moreover, this aspect comprises a form of communication that explores emotional responses and stimuli while renouncing rationality or fact-based argumentation.

These aspects have been examined in the study conducted by Hernández-Santaolalla and Sola-Morales (2019) regarding the 2017 Catalan process[1], where the authors analysed 573 tweets published around the voting date. Their study revealed the tendency of politicians to follow rhetorical discursive strategies based on emotion and feelings. Regarding social media users' response, the authors identified the trend to resort more to an aggressive approach towards divergent viewpoints and less rational debates of ideas.

Another study that examined political public opinion was conducted by Torbisco Cervantes and Gomero Correa (2021) in Peru, addressing 150 offensive comments published on Facebook in September 2020. They were triggered by discriminatory expressions articulated by the congresswoman Martha Chávez against Peru's former prime minister Vicente Zeballos. According to the local press (Perú21, 2020), in order to express her disagreement with the appointment of Vicente Zeballos as Peru's representative at OAS (Organization of American States), the congresswoman would have said that 'he should [instead] have gone to Bolivia as a Moqueguano and as a person with Andean features'.

The study shows that one of the most problematic aspects of political statements of this nature comprises the fact that they generate a ripple effect of subsequent demeaning manifestations of a series of social media comments that disseminate and reinforce white supremacist ideologies. Within it, Torbisco

---

[1] This process comprises an independence referendum held on 01 October 2017 in the Spanish autonomous community of Catalonia, whose results revealed 92% in support for the independence and 8% against. However, on 17 October 2017, the referendum law was declared void by the Spanish government.

Cervantes and Gomero Correa (2021) argue that expressing racism with the association of white supremacy remains latent, where whiteness and racial exclusion, coupled with racial and cultural racism, are reinforced. Moreover, the authors continue saying that the perception or belief in white privilege leads to indigenous traits being regarded as inferior or negative features compared to European ones (i.e., white features). Finally, social media is contributing to making racism visible.

What is also important to highlight is the fact that both aspects raised by Torbisco Cervantes and Gomero Correa (2021) and the discriminatory statement made by the Peruvian congresswoman are also observed in other South American countries. In this regard, Solano Rivera and Ramírez Caro (2019) bring the following examples: a) in Argentina, the former president Mauricio Macri once claimed that 'in South America, we are all European descendants'; b) in Brazil, the former president Jair Bolsonaro boasted that his son 'was well-educated and would never fall in love with a Black woman'; and c) in Colombia, the former president Iván Duque said that 'most of the country's criminals are Black, and even if you provide free education to them, I doubt they will get out of poverty, because they are lazy'.

Thus, the statements as mentioned above ignore and neglect any relevant role played by Africans and indigenous communities in forming South American societies, disqualifying them and removing their humanity and social value. On top of that, since those individuals are prominent and influential public figures in their respective countries, they endorse, and legitimate white supremacist discourses fostered by social media users.

Another distinctive aspect to take into consideration is the fact that not only key political figures such as Donald Trump, Jair Bolsonaro, and Matteo Salvini have explored social media to convey their nationalist political views, as explained by Trindade (2020c), but also political parties. In Spain, the young far-right political party Vox (established in 2013 when social media was already a reality) represents an interesting example. According to a study conducted by Castro Martínez and Díaz Morilla (2021), at a discursive level, Vox employs emotional arguments, appealing to feelings such as fear (mainly concerning immigrants, communism and left-wing politicians). Their 'enemies' are defined as the press, political opponents, and immigrants, who, combined, become the focus of criticism, disqualification, and ridicule. Finally, the authors explain, Vox applies demeaning language that highlights patriotic feelings and sense of belonging, combined with visual communication strategies typical of social media (e.g., meme, short videos that are easy to share through smartphones, filters, emoticons, etc.).

### Deep-rooted and enduring racism

An ample and robust literature reveals that Latin American countries share a common history of long-lasting European colonialism (especially from Spain and Portugal, but also France, the Netherlands, and the UK in smaller proportions). This process has brought a series of enduring negative legacies across the continent, including, for example, frequent political instability, deep and enduring economic inequalities, profound racial hierarchies that afford privileges to whites to the detriment of other ethnicities and racial groups, and structural racism (Gibson, 1963; Stern, 1985; Ryan, 1999; van Dijk, 2005; Wade, 2010).

Then, what concerns the phenomenon of racism, it is relevant to explain that it stands for a social system of domination of one hegemonic social group (in this case, white European colonizers) over other non-European social groups (i.e., indigenous communities and enslaved African individuals), built on top of differences of ethnicity, place of origin, culture, religion, and language (van Dijk, 2005).

Thus, having introduced this brief and necessary contextual explanation, it is possible to observe that the sample of studies in Spanish reveals that enduring racism in Latin America is also widespread on social media. Amidst it, Carrillo Urcid (2020) has conducted a study examining racist discourses disseminated on Facebook and Twitter in Mexico, aiming to identify how these discriminatory discursive strategies are fostered. First, the author has found that a single comment or image is enough to trigger a long thread of subsequent comments that easily escalate to increasingly aggressive language.

Secondly, given the high accessibility of social media in Mexico, which has become the space where racism is openly verbalised, even if sometimes the discourses might be concealed in informal 'plays', they are still there. Finally, given the colonial legacy, as previously mentioned, Carrillo Urcid (2020) has also found that racial hierarchy dynamics (i.e., whiteness is praised, while blackness, indigenous, and mestizos are disqualified) plays a significant role in the construction of the discriminatory discourses.

It is also important to explain that a social phenomenon like racism is not unidimensional and is usually intertwined with several other equally complex phenomena, such as xenophobia, religious intolerance, sexism, and so forth (Bustos Martínez *et al.*, 2019). Within this line of reasoning, it is possible to observe that Arana Castañeda (2020) reveals the role played by COVID-19 in Colombia, triggering racist discourses on Facebook.

The numerous uncertainties raised with the advent of COVID-19 contributed to creating varying degrees of panic and fear across many societies around the globe. Within it, there were several episodes of quest for a scapegoat and someone to blame for the emergence of the pandemic. In the case of Colombia, Arana Castañeda (2020) argues that dark skin colour and belonging to a certain geographic location (the *Aguablanca* district in Cali) became the catalyst for a series of derogatory narratives and negative social representations of the inhabitants of that area.

According to the author, the individuals belonging to the *Aguablanca* district (mostly comprised of lower-class Afro-descendants) were labelled as responsible for the harmful effects of the pandemic. Then, fuelled by a colonial-like perspective of racial hierarchy, Arana Castañeda (2020) has identified that social media users have constructed racialised social representations and narratives about the *Aguablanca* community that separate them from the 'good citizens' of Colombia, which means that they are not 'one of us' (i.e., the hegemonic whitened social group).

Indeed, it is possible to notice that the colonial legacy that fuels this pernicious logic of inclusion *vs* exclusion and privilege *vs* marginalisation seems to be very strong in Latin American countries. Another supporting example of this claim is present in the study conducted by Mejía Núñez (2022) exploring 'humorous' posts published on the *Cosas de Whitexicans* Twitter account.

In essence, the posts published on this Twitter account employ humour to conceal racist ideologies and play with the ambivalence of what they consider to be genuinely white Mexican (i.e., upper class, better housing conditions, superior, better schooling, and so forth) and, by contrast, whatever is deemed of reduced value or negative is associated with lower class Afro-descendant, indigenous, and mestizos (Mejía Núñez, 2022).

Then, reflecting on the decisive role played by modern means of communication in Colombia, including social media platforms like Facebook and Twitter, Arriaga Arango (2013) advocates that they have become characterised by the capability of disseminating and conveying a variety of stereotypes about Black people. In alignment with this reflection, Ferrándiz *et al.* (2011) also argue that in Peru, although the manifestations of racism and social exclusion are not restricted solely to the virtual environment, it is through them that discriminatory discourses can be more easily disseminated. The authors say that given the powerful networking capabilities of social media platforms like Facebook and Twitter, they afford people to freely unleash a series of discriminatory ideologies that can easily escalate and even trigger aggressive behaviour.

### Other social issues

Similar to what was observed in the sample of studies published in Portuguese, in Spanish, is also possible to find a group of studies exploring various social issues. However, as previously mentioned, the interconnection among the varied social phenomena cannot be disregarded.

One of such issues comprises the construction and dissemination of discourses on Facebook in Peru opposing gender ideology, as investigated by Meneses (2019). In this particular study calls attention to the fact that one should expect that anti-gender ideology discourses would be triggered or influenced by conservative political leaders. Nonetheless, Meneses (2019) explores the issue from an innovative religious perspective.

In other words, the author argues that a cohort of religious individuals in a Peruvian Facebook community, established in opposition to the gender ideology, has exercised their power of influence like pastors in charge of guiding their followers away from the gender ideology 'perdition' and towards 'salvation'. Consequently, the author continues, this discursive strategy praises normative values such as heterosexuality in direct opposition to LGBTQI+ individuals. Thus, it means to say that to oppose gender ideology, the discourses are built on top of conservative religious moral values.

Evolving from this reflection, it is possible to observe that also in El Salvador, conservative discourses on social media have been constructed and disseminated in opposition to the LGBTQI+ community. In this case, Arévalo and Duarte (2018, p. 44) explain that "in contemporary society, sexual and political identities such as lesbian, gay, trans people, bisexuals or intersex (LGBTI), named as *homesexualistas* by the conservative discourses direct their political agenda of hate and discrimination".

In their study, the authors have identified two types of discourses: 1) *hardcore*, which is characterised as recognising the silence-taboo and public insults as cultural discursive devices to legitimise discrimination processes, and 2) *light*, which is represented by 'friendly' homophobia as a discursive strategy and political weapon that triggers categories such as affection, tolerance, charity, and fostering to deny and reject any type of recognition of rights for Salvadorian LGBTI community (Arévalo and Duarte, 2018).

Then, while the two previous studies have focused on the intersectionality of gender and sexual orientation in Peru and El Salvador, Sepúlveda Logorreta and Flores Treviño (2019) have investigated sexist discourses on Facebook in Mexico, exploring the intersection of gender, class, and ethnicity. According to Wade (2010), in the project to position Latin American countries in the modernity era at the beginning of the twentieth century, the dominant elites of the continent aimed to emulate the European standard of modernity and progress. However, this model of modernity and progress had no room for Blacks and indigenous communities since they represent backwardness and deviance.

Thus, the sexist discriminatory discourses against female indigenous individuals on Facebook in Mexico are, in fact, a reflection of this historical legacy. Amidst it, the analysis of 150 Facebook comments conducted by Sepúlveda Logorreta and Flores Treviño (2019) reveals that the discourses tend to reflect acts of impoliteness and the predominance of insults and threats to the image of indigenous women performing the role of public civil servants. In other words, in addition to sexism, this sort of discursive strategy also represents manifestations of power, dominance, and superiority.

As can be noticed in the present chapter through the analysis of some of the studies published in Spanish, different from what is observed in the studies published in Portuguese, societal issues involving indigenous communities are quite present (Sepúlveda Logorreta and Flores Treviño, 2019; Torbisco Cervantes and Gomero Correa, 2021; Mejía Núñez, 2022). A plausible explanation for this relevant aspect lays in the fact that despite the near extermination of the indigenous communities due to the colonisation process, in several Latin American countries, the proportion of native peoples' descendants is still relatively high, as revealed by van Dijk (2005): a) Belize: 14.7%, b) Bolivia: 56.8%, c) Ecuador: 29.5%, d) Guatemala: 43.8%, e) Mexico: 14.2%, f) Nicaragua: 14.25%, g) Peru: 40.8%, and finally, the total in the continent is 14.76%. The proportion in Latin America is not higher than the overall figure just presented because, in Brazil, the current indigenous population accounts for just 1.6 million people (equivalent to 0.74% of the country's population), in contrast to an estimate of up to 5 million people in the sixteenth century when the Portuguese colonisers arrived in the land (Azevedo, 2008; Gandra, 2023).

In this way, the study conducted by Bagua (2020) explores the social representation of indigenous people on Twitter in Ecuador and, more specifically, regarding an indigenous man who was leading a football team (*Mushuc Runa Sporting Club*) which had obtained a historical classification to participate in the 2019 edition of the *Copa Sudamericana*.

Among the findings of this research, what stands out is the argument advocated by Bagua (2020), which says that over more than five centuries, the hegemonic power in Ecuador has fostered a discriminatory collective memory that is manifested in discourses, popular stories and narratives, texts, and renewed images built on top of outdated perceptions of time, space, gender, and ethnicity. Ultimately, this dynamic justifies seeing the 'other' and their symbolic universe as inferior, as something to be known, civilised, and incorporated into the structure and logic of power.

Another distinctive aspect worth mentioning is that while some authors have explored the issue of hate speech in general without focusing on any specific type of hate speech (Campillo Muñoz, 2019; Arcila Calderón *et al.*, 2020; Zuban and Rabbia, 2021; Oña-Arcentales *et al.*, 2022; Parodi *et al.*, 2022), one study in particular calls the attention for addressing an underexplored social issue. That is, the subject matter of *fanbullying*, as investigated by Vizcaíno-Verdú *et al.* (2020).

According to the authors, fanbullying stands for the pernicious relationship between fans and famous actors/actresses[2] on social media, meaning that users demonstrate abusive behaviour towards prominent actors/actresses online. The study was conducted in the Spanish social context, and the authors have identified that, often, aggressive social media users are unable to distinguish between the actor/actress as a citizen and the role they play or the character they represent. It is all too blurry for them, and everything is merged. Then, as explained by Vizcaíno-Verdú *et al.* (2020), the individuals who engage in the practice of fanbullying through the dissemination of aggressive and derogatory comments aim to trigger a response from the victims, which in turn might provide the bullies with a sense of self-affirmation, attract many like-minded users and even grant them some sort of 'prestige' within their online community.

### Overview of the social media platforms most examined

Different from what is observed in the studies published in Portuguese, the sample of studies published in Spanish show a high concentration of Facebook and Twitter, which combined represent 83.3% of the studies, while the remaining 16.7% is scattered among other social media platforms.

To a certain extent, it can be said that this high concentration is relatively surprising, especially because Facebook enjoys a leadership position across Spanish-speaking countries, while Twitter is much less popular (see Table 5.1).

On the other hand, it is also a fact that the manifestations of hate speech and intolerance often occur on these two platforms. Moreover, it is also possible that authors might experience fewer technical obstacles to obtaining research data compared to other platforms.

In addition, this picture also shows the potential for future studies in Spanish exploring various platforms such as Instagram, YouTube, and WhatsApp, adopting both qualitative and quantitative methodological approaches.

---

[2] Although there are voices in favour of using 'actor' both for male and female professionals, in the present book it has been chosen to employ 'actor and actress' because, given the lack of consensus, this choice is in alignment with the approach still adopted by the world's most famous, influential, and prestigious acting awards, the Oscars (https://www.oscars.org/oscars/ceremonies/2023).

# Chapter 6

# Analysis of studies published in Italian

*"Not everything that is faced can be changed,*
*but nothing can be changed until it is faced".*

(James Baldwin)

## Introduction

Consistent with the previous two chapters, the present one also starts with an overview of the social media landscape in Italy. Subsequently, the sample of 18 studies were examined, again following an iterative process of interrogation to allow the emergence of key themes (Jorgensen and Phillips, 2002). This approach has led to the identification of four prevailing themes: 1) the interplay between COVID-19 and infodemics, 2) hate speech and resistance, 3) xenophobia and cyberbullying, and 4) revenge porn and gendered hate speech.

The chapter finishes then with a brief section commenting on the prevailing social media platforms examined in the Italian studies.

## Overview of social media landscape in Italy

Concerning the general profile of social media users in Italy, it is possible to notice a certain degree of similarity with Spanish-speaking countries analysed in the present study, since the proportion of male and female users is practically even (see Table 6.1). On the other hand, as previously discussed in Chapter 4, Brazil and Portugal show some of the highest proportion of female users.

Another aspect that emerges from the data displayed in Table 6.1 comprises the evidence that among the 11 countries represented in the sample of studies, Italy shows the fourth largest proportion of social media users in relation to the country's population (74.5%). This metric is relevant because it contributes to understanding social media's ubiquitousness in Italian society. On the other hand, it also calls attention to the fact that, also among the 11 countries in the sample, Italian users are the ones who spend less time using the technology (just 1h 48min per day), and also well below the global average of 2h 31min.

Nonetheless, as the diverse studies analysed in the present chapter reveal, this reduced time spent on social media does not mean the absence of construction and dissemination of a myriad of manifestations of hate speech and intolerance. On the opposite, those phenomena affect the lives of a number of people in Italy the same way it is observed in other social contexts.

**Table 6.1**: Summary of social media data in Italy

| Country and Metrics | | Italy |
|---|---|---|
| Country's Population (million) | | 58.96 |
| Active Social Media Users (million) | | 43.9 |
| Relative in Relation to the Population | | 74.5% |
| Time Spent Using Social Media | | 1h 48min |
| World Averagee | | 2h 31min |
| Social Media Users | Male | 50.1% |
| | Female | 49.9% |
| Most Used Social Media Platforms | Facebook | 77.5% |
| | FB Messenger | 50.6% |
| | Instagram | 72.9% |
| | Telegram | 46.5% |
| | TikTok | 37.5% |
| | Twitter | 26.4% |
| | WhatsApp | 89.9% |

Source: The author, based on Kemp (2023i)

Besides, another data that stands out from Table 6.1 comprises the reduced users' preference for Facebook (just 77.5%, while just Spain shows a lower figure with 72.5%). In contrast, Facebook enjoys users' preference of at least 83.3% in Portugal and up to 92.9% in Mexico. On the other hand, similarly to what is observed across the other 10 countries analysed, WhatsApp also enjoys a leadership position in Italy. However, despite these different figures, it cannot be disregarded the fact that Facebook, FB Messenger, Instagram, and WhatsApp all belong to the same Meta corporation. Consequently, by the end of the day, the observed difference in users' preference across the 11 countries does not significantly change the overall landscape since the upper position on the podium is always occupied by the same entity (i.e., Meta) that is capable of setting the trends in the global industry of social media platforms and influence the rules of the game.

Finally, concerning the studies published in Italian, as previously addressed in Chapter 3, most of the scholarly papers in the sample have been published within the past five to six years (see Figure 3.2). The explanation for this aspect has already been discussed in the same Chapter 3 and, although, to a certain extent, it can be viewed as an unintentional limitation of the study, it has, in reality, become a strength. That is because the sample of studies published in Italian addresses a variety of topics not very present in the studies published in Portuguese and Spanish. Moreover, they also cover more recent issues, such as the COVID-19 pandemic, infodemics, cyberbullying, and the phenomenon of revenge porn.

## Main themes emerged from the sample of studies

### *The interplay between COVID-19 and infodemics*

From early January 2020, news began to circulate regarding a new respiratory disease caused by a virus and that the first city to be strongly affected was Wuhan in China. In a matter of four to eight weeks, the virus had reached other Asian countries, Europe and, later on, the Americas (Taylor, 2020). Within this overall context, in addition to becoming a global public health emergency, it has also contributed to the exacerbation of various social phenomena like racism, discrimination, xenophobia, and other manifestations of intolerance.

Hence, based on this premise, it is possible to observe that Pasta *et al.* (2021) have conducted an investigation aimed at understanding the possible surge of antisemitism on Twitter triggered by the emergence of COVID-19. Bearing in mind that the literature reveals that China comprised the first country severely affected by the disease, it can be said that the focus of this research conducted by Pasta *et al.* (2021) might seem relatively unusual. However, the authors explain that a 2020 report entitled *Coronavirus and the Plague of Antisemitism*, published by the London-based *Community Security Trust*, warned about four main aspects: 1) the virus is fake and a Jewish conspiracy, 2) the virus is real but even so it is the outcome of a plot, 3) the virus has a life on its own, but Jews spread it, and 4) the virus should be directed against Jews.

Nonetheless, despite the aspects raised in the British report, the study conducted by Pasta *et al.* (2021) did not reveal a surge of antisemitism hate speech on Twitter triggered by the emergence of COVID-19. This evidence is understandable and makes sense because another Italian study conducted by Cologna (2020) had already suggested a surge of Sinophobia rather than antisemitism, which coalesces with other studies such as Chandra (2020), Rafi (2020), Schild *et al.* (2020) and more recently Trindade and Acevedo (2023).

In this way, it is possible to observe that COVID-19 also triggered another worrisome social phenomenon coined as infodemics. According to Caliandro *et al.* (2020, p. 175), "infodemics stands for a sudden epidemic of disinformation that spreads rapidly through the internet and social media, posing serious threats to public health". Thus, the authors say, infodemics is intrinsically linked with the phenomenon of fake news. Within it, is interesting to notice that disinformation is not simply the mere conscious dissemination of inaccurate information but the construction of news and information that looks true, legitimate and reliable. That is, they are framed in real contexts but merged with fake or distorted data, unreliable or made-up sources, manipulated facts and induce the receiver to believe they are trustworthy (Barreto Junior, 2022). Moreover, social media platforms represent the most convenient vehicle for disseminating fake news because they allow people to spread them instantaneously and reach a wide audience.

Additionally, it is also ironic to discuss the phenomenon of massification of fake news and infodemics when social media has also normalised the use of the adjective 'viral' to refer to content that spreads rapidly, replicates widely and out of control, just like the COVID-19 pandemic.

However, despite these conceptual explanations, in the case of the study mentioned above conducted by Caliandro *et al.* (2020), analysing 7.2 million tweets, the authors did not find a scenario of infodemics in Italy. Instead, they have found a predominance of fake news associating coronavirus diffusion and immigration, which, according to the authors, does not threaten public health. Furthermore, the authors say that this scenario is linked to far-right political discourses aimed at strengthening their anti-immigration political agenda.

On the other hand, it is possible to notice that Lovari and Righetti (2020) have a different view and understand that the context of COVID-19 in Italy represented a favourable background for disseminating infodemics. Not by chance, according to the authors, the Ministry of Health has implemented a series of communication strategies on Facebook to combat disinformation and fake news circulating on Italian social media.

The study has analysed 459 Facebook posts published by the Ministry of Health and identified, first, a predominance of visual communication methods (i.e., infographics) to convey reliable information to citizens in a very didactic and clear way. Secondly, most of the posts were reactive rather than proactive (i.e., they were focused on debunking specific fake news circulating online), while another portion was aimed at raising public awareness (e.g., encouraging the use of surgical masks, respecting social distance, etc.) and reinforcing the importance of following just official information provided by the authorities (Lovari and Righetti, 2020).

### Hate speech and resistance

As previously seen in the studies published both in Portuguese and Spanish, hate speech on social media represents a global phenomenon and the subject of concern among several international organisations. In this scenario, the studies published in Italian also corroborate this picture.

Amidst it, the study conducted by Bentivegna and Rega (2020) aimed at investigating not only hateful discourses (i.e., the message) but other dimensions such as the communicator, the receiver, and the digital media (i.e., the vehicle). Thus, adopting a sociological-communicative perspective, the authors explain that rather than seeing hate speech merely as a pathological discourse or a deviant behaviour to be banned or censored, they have instead considered hate speech in terms of a communicative process. Consequently, the analysis of the hate speech phenomenon should consider the interaction among the diverse elements involved, encompassing the source, the message, the audience, and the means (Bentivegna and Rega, 2020).

Then, while it is more common to find studies emphasising the characteristics and potential harms of hate speech (e.g., Milicia, 2016; Bortone and Cerquozzi, 2017; Fumagalli, 2019), it is possible to notice that Santerini (2019) brings a different perspective by focusing on resistance initiatives. In this context, the author advocates that nowadays, the most important task for different social agents concerned with hate speech is not restricted to warnings regarding their impact. Instead, it is imperative to strengthen anti-hate education and foster factual counter-narratives that challenge disinformation, fake news, and hate speech (Santerini, 2019).

### Xenophobia and cyberbullying

It is interesting to notice that similar to what is observed in the sample of studies published in Spanish, the subject of immigration, although in a smaller proportion, is also present in the sample of studies in Italian, which is understandable since immigration comprises a prominent social concern among several European countries. Moreover, Italy is one of the first points of arrival for North African immigrants arriving from the Mediterranean Sea who wish to enter Europe.

Consequently, the intertwined relation between conservative political discourses and negative or stereotypical portrayals of immigrants on social media also becomes clear. In this context, Nicolosi (2019) highlights the dangers of using immigration as a symbolic resource for political communication, which fosters a climate of collective 'moral panic' and justifies implementing very restrictive measures by anti-immigration policymakers. Besides, the author also shows how the stratification of these policies can lead to mass structural violence, which is sustained and legitimised by symbolic and cultural violence.

Then, in another study, Zannoni (2017) addresses the issue of intolerance and xenophobic hate speech on Facebook (especially targeted against North African immigrants), which has become a serious subject of educational concern regarding the young population. The author highlights the dark side of the internet and Facebook, which includes multiple racist, xenophobic and antisemitic content, alongside incitement to hate and hostility towards ethnic minorities. Furthermore, still according to the author, social media platforms from the mid-2000s onwards have contributed to amplifying these phenomena.

Thus, to challenge this scenario, Zannoni (2017) advocates that, educational initiatives must be implemented to respond to this issue by promoting a perspective based on pluralism, dialogue, active listening, and tolerance, which the author calls 'pedagogy of interculturality'.

To a certain extent, it is possible to notice that the argument advocated by Zannoni (2017) overlaps with another study conducted by Cera (2017), who has reviewed 12 scholarly articles exploring the relationship among school, family, adolescents, and social media. Then, based on this literature review, the author aims to demonstrate the importance of a mediation role of families in educating youngsters on digital literacy based on explaining, clarifying, and demonstrating to them the potential risks involved with the use of social media.

Besides, it can also be said that the debate proposed by Cera (2017) and Zannoni (2017) is important because it can be linked with the phenomenon of cyberbullying, bearing in mind that young people comprise the biggest demographic group targeted by bullies on social media (Rega and Lovari, 2019). In the study, the authors examine this abusive behaviour (i.e., cyberbullying) within a broader framework that connects bullying to the growth of incivility in public discourse. Finally, Rega and Lovari (2019) identify recurring dimensions in cyberbullying, including the repetition of the gesture, the imbalance of power, and the intention and aggressiveness that differs from 'ordinary' offline aggression.

Based in these studies, it is possible to understand that five key elements characterise the phenomenon of cyberbullying: a) the intention to explore somebody else's characteristics deemed 'deviant' or 'different' before the eyes of the abusers and cause harm, b) an audience who passively whiteness the abusive behaviour and, on several occasions, also engages in bullying, which contributes to amplifying its reach and impact on the victim, c) the anonymity of the person who engages in the practice of bullying, since oftentimes they try hiding their identity, d) the repetition of this abusive behaviour, in such a way that the more they engage in this practice, the more it becomes naturalised, and e) in most bullying circumstances, the abuser wants to exercise their power and enforce their self-perceived superiority over vulnerable people.

Finally, the combination of these key elements brings serious negative impacts in people's lives. Examples of such negative consequences include, but are not restricted to: panic syndrome, depression, lack of self-esteem, losing self-confidence, self-isolation, among many others.

### Revenge porn and gendered hate speech

As already mentioned in the present study, most of the time, it is difficult to separate the phenomena in individual analytical 'boxes', taking into account that they often overlap and are interconnected. In the case of the phenomenon of revenge porn and misogyny, the interconnection is blatant, and it is practically impossible to attempt to address them separately.

In this regard, Gattamelata (2022) explains that revenge porn comprises the practice of publishing, on the internet or social media, sexualised (often explicit) or intimate images of the ex-partner without their prior knowledge or consent. The aim is to humiliate the person through public shame by the inappropriate exposition of such graphic images. Still, according to Gattamelata (2022), nine out of ten victims are female (ranging from adolescents to mature women).

The most common triggering event behind this practice is a breakup, which is not easily accepted or received by the male partner, who strongly believes that he has the right to 'punish' the female (ex-)partner. However, a deeper analysis of this phenomenon reveals that men (both young and adult) who engage in this practice want to enforce their power, reinforce their masculinity, and delegitimise the women's 'audacity' in challenging male's dominance and control in a romantic relationship.

Ultimately, as argued by Gattamelata (2022), revenge porn invades the most intimate sphere of the subject without their consent, and due to that, some voices call this practice a sort of 'cyber rape'. The very serious violation of one's privacy and the unrestricted public exposure of their intimacy lead to a series of painful experiences that can be very difficult to heal. Furthermore, the authors add that around 50% of the victims reveal that revenge porn has exposed them to embarrassing and unpleasant circumstances of harassment and stalking by unknown individuals that saw their photos and videos on social media.

In alignment with these arguments, Abbatecola (2021) is another author in the sample of studies in Italian who highlights the harmful impacts of revenge porn, whose victims are mostly women. However, the author's main objective comprises a critical reflection regarding the terminology 'revenge porn', which she considers inappropriate, and the proposes a new one, 'D.I.V.I.S.E.', which stands for *Diffusione Illicita di Video e Immagini Sessualmente Esplicite*[1] (Abbatecola, 2021).

The author recognises that the proposed acronym might not be as 'catchy' or immediately understood, as is the case with revenge porn. But, on the other hand, the author also considers that the continuation of the use of the terminology revenge porn reinforces the very aggressive male-dominated culture it seeks to combat, and that a more nuanced and intersectional approach is needed to address the phenomenon of non-consensual sharing of intimate images.

Then, it is possible to notice that, in complement to these reflections, Spallaccia (2018) has conducted a study to call attention to gender-based hate speech both on the internet in general and on social media, which, according to the author, although women have been increasingly targeted, there still a gap in the literature.

In support of her argumentation, the author suggests that interdisciplinary synergy is necessary to investigate gender-based hate speech's impact on contemporary societies' cultural advancement. Finally, in-depth studies in this direction are desirable to identify educational and even legal measures aimed at promoting correct and non-discriminatory use of digital technologies, such as the internet and social media, and enabling the creation of a civil society capable of guaranteeing the right to expression as participation to all its members (Spallaccia, 2018).

### Overview of the social media platforms most examined

In alignment with what is observed in most of the literature in the discipline of social media studies, the platforms most examined are Facebook and Twitter, despite their significant differences in users' preference in Italy (77.5% *vs* 26.4%, respectively).

Nonetheless, two other aspects call attention in the sample of studies in Italian. First, several studies did not focus on any specific social media but rather address them on general terms (i.e., 31.8% say simply 'social media') and, secondly, other authors have explored hate speech and intolerance on the

---

[1] Illegal Dissemination of Sexually Explicit Videos and Images

internet broadly speaking, which in some cases also include social media, while others they have not specified.

Finally, it is also relevant to mention the absence of studies exploring Instagram, YouTube, and WhatsApp, which are very successful and popular platforms in Italy and worldwide. Thus, this aspect also reveals a gap in the literature in Italian and the big potential for future studies.

# Chapter 7

# Cross-cultural analysis of hate speech

*"I would like to tell you all this personally, to be able to see your face as I speak to you, and for you to see mine. I enjoy writing to you very much but looking at you as I speak to you is like reading you twice".*

(Vera Vidal Romero)

## Introduction

The review of the sample of 108 scholarly papers developed in the previous three chapters has revealed interesting aspects across diverse countries. First, in the case of **studies published in Portuguese**, the main themes emerged from the sample of 51 studies comprised: 1) the intersection of gender, race and class, 2) politically motivated hate speech, 3) homophobic hate speech, and 4) social representation and xenophobic discourses.

As already explained in Chapter 4, one of the unintentional limitations of the study comprises the reduced number of scholarly papers published in Portugal and, consequently, the findings of this chapter reflect more the Brazilian scenario.

In this context, it is possible to notice that the varied types of hate speech represented in the aforementioned main themes, reflect that social context. In the case of *the intersection of gender, race and class*, the studies analysed reveal that the manifestations of hate speech are fuelled by aspects such as heteronormative white superiority, deep-rooted racism, a patriarchal social context, and the users' need to reinforce their masculinity (Stocker and Dalmaso, 2016; Silveira-Barbosa and Rocha, 2018; Martins, 2019).

In the case of *politically motivated hate speech*, it is possible to observe that hate speech became more prominent with the increasing polarising political tensions between far-right political forces *vs* progressive parties within the past two decades. Indeed, several studies reviewed in the chapter have addressed this aspect (Maia and Rezende, 2015; Wainberg and Müller, 2017; Carvalho *et al.*, 2018).

Regarding *homophobic hate speech*, in a certain way, also involves elements of gender discrimination, but what prevails in the motivational factors behind this type of hate speech are the reinforcement of heteronormative values (Silva,

2018), masculinity (Alves and Paulo, 2017), and the dissemination of normative values in opposition to other considered 'deviant' (Silva and Aléssio, 2019; Silva *et al.*, 2020; Silva and Silva, 2021).

What concerns *social representation and xenophobic discourses* on Brazilian social media, the sample of studies reveals that social representation is strongly influenced by racist ideologies that praise whiteness as the ultimate symbol of progress, modernity, intelligence, beauty, and higher moral standards while disqualifying blackness and associate it with a series of negative attributes (Luz, 2019; Silva, 2020b). As with xenophobic discourses, although Brazil usually does not receive the same proportion of immigrants as seen in the US and some European countries, the anti-immigration political rhetoric and general population's negative sentiment are the same. In other words, the immigrants are oftentimes depicted and perceived as 'invaders' and considered undesirable people (Moura and Souza, 2019; Seara and Cabral, 2020).

Evolving to the **studies published in Spanish** (Chapter 5), it was possible to observe the emergence of three main themes: 1) xenophobic discourses, 2) politically motivated hate speech, and 3) deep-rooted and enduring racism. Here is interesting to notice some similarities and differences in comparison to the main themes emerged from the studies published in Portuguese.

To begin with, it is possible to notice that *xenophobic hate speech* has been more present in the studies published in Spanish, since they are fuelled by diverse conflicting circumstances. In this regard, it calls attention to aspects such as a caravan of Central American immigrants heading towards the US but passing through Mexico and subjected to a series of xenophobic discourses on social media (Reyes Vázquez and Barrios de la O, 2019; Pérez Díaz and Aguilar Pérez, 2021).

Moreover, challenging political, social, and economic circumstances have driven the immigration of Venezuelan citizens to neighbouring countries such as Ecuador and Peru, but have also exposed them to numerous episodes of xenophobic discourses on social media in both countries (Altamirano and Torres-Toukoumidis, 2021; Vega, 2022). Besides, xenophobic hate speech has also targeted Nicaraguans in Costa Rica (Solano Rivera and Ramírez Caro, 2019) and immigrants arriving by boat in Spain (Fernández Fernández *et al.*, 2020).

Ultimately, as seen in the studies published in Portuguese (Moura and Souza, 2019; Seara and Cabral, 2020), the hateful xenophobic discourses are fuelled by defence mechanisms employed by hegemonic social groups to safeguard their established positions and protect resources that they perceive to be threatened by the arrival of 'invaders' (i.e., immigrants).

What concerns the *politically motivated hate speech*, similar to what was observed in Brazil, this type of hate speech in Spanish-speaking countries is also triggered by strong political polarisation and the emergence of far-right political forces in the recent past (Cerna Aragón, 2017; Hernández-Santaolalla and Sola-Morales, 2019; Torbisco Cervantes and Gomero Correa, 2021).

In alignment with what has been revealed in the studies in Portuguese, the representatives of far-right political forces and their supporters tend to convey not only conservative ideals, but also discourses of higher moral standards than their political rivals. Additionally, in many circumstances, they depict their political opponents as enemies rather than competitors. This factor is important because it is not a simple matter of semantics but is has the potential do influence their behaviour regarding people who think different from them.

As with *deep-rooted racism* in Spanish-speaking countries, it is possible to observe a natural and expected high degree of alignment with the overall Brazilian context because, as revealed in the literature, Latin American countries share a series of common negative legacies of European colonization (van Dijk, 2005; Wade, 2010).

Nonetheless, what is different in the studies published in Spanish comprises the fact that oftentimes, the target of hate speech tends to be individuals of indigenous origins (Sepúlveda Logorreta and Flores Treviño, 2019; Torbisco Cervantes and Gomero Correa, 2021; Mejía Núñez, 2022). However, despite the diverse general profile of the predominant victims of racist hate speech in Brazil (Black individuals) and other Latin American countries (mostly members of indigenous communities), the supporting ideology fuelling the discriminatory discourses is the same (i.e., white supremacy).

Evolving to the sample of **studies published in Italian** (Chapter 6), four main themes have emerged from the sample of 18 scholarly papers: 1) the interplay between COVID-19 and infodemics, 2) hates speech and resistance, 3) xenophobia and cyberbullying, and 4) revenge porn and gendered hate speech.

The first aspect that stands out in this list of themes, is the fact that it differs considerably in comparison with the studies published in Portuguese and Spanish, albeit keeping a few similarities (i.e., xenophobia).

Since Italy was among the first Western countries to be severely affected by the emergence of COVID-19 pandemic in early 2020, this aspect has contributed to the development of a certain level of collective panic fuelled by high levels of uncertainty, and the search for scapegoats. The combination of these sentiments has triggered not only manifestations of hate speech but, as the studies revealed, the worrisome spread of disinformation, which has been coined as *infodemics* (Caliandro *et al.*, 2020; Cologna, 2020; Pasta *et al.*, 2021).

This infodemics phenomenon is very problematic because, similar to fake news, users engaged in their construction and dissemination merge real facts with distorted or unreliable data, and with that, they induce the receiver to believe they are trustworthy (Barreto Junior, 2022).

What concerns the study of *hate speech*, it is interesting to observe that Bentivegna and Rega (2020) propose the examination of the phenomenon beyond the discourses on social media and advocate a more holistic perspective. Thus, according to the authors, studies should encompass a broader array of elements, such as the source, the message, the audience, and the means. On the other hand, Santerini (2019) highlights *resistance* initiatives fostered on social media, such as anti-hate education and counter-narratives capable of challenging disinformation, fake news and hate speech.

Then, what concerns *xenophobic discourses* on social media, the studies published in Italian (Zannoni, 2017; Nicolosi, 2019) coalesce with the ones published in Spanish, in the sense that the discriminatory ideologies triggering the hateful discourses are the same (i.e., the portrayal of immigrants as 'invaders' threatening the established positions and resources of the hegemonic social group).

Another unique theme that emerged from the Italian studies comprises the abusive behaviour of cyberbullying, whose main victims are usually young users (Cera, 2017; Rega and Lovari, 2019). The reason for that lies in the fact that young people comprise the biggest demographic group using digital technologies. Since they tend to spend long hours per month online, they are also prone to being exposed to inappropriate content.

The fourth theme emerged from the sample of studies in Italian, *revenge porn and gendered hate speech*, combines some unique characteristics. First, it is clear that gender dimension comprises a core element in this type of hate speech. Second, it reinforces findings from other studies (Erjavec and Kovačič, 2012; Trindade, 2018), in the sense that male users are the ones most prone to be involved in cases of hate speech on social media. Consequently, this aspect leads towards the third characteristic of this type of hate speech: the effort to maintain and enforce ideals of power imbalance between men and women and also the reinforcement of their masculinity (Spallaccia, 2018; Abbatecola, 2021; Gattamelata, 2022).

Therefore, to sum up, it is possible to observe from this cross-cultural analysis, that while a series of country-specific themes have emerged from the sample of studies, there has been also some degree of overlapping. But, in essence, they reveal that, despite differences in historical backgrounds across the 11 countries represented in the sample, certain discriminatory and intolerant ideologies are transcultural and permeate varied types of hateful discourses (e.g., racist, xenophobic, misogynistic, and politically motivated hate speech).

### The societal impacts of hate speech and abusive behaviour

After examining the cross-cultural aspects of the sample of 108 scholarly papers in the previous section, it is considered a coherent further step to question what sort of societal impacts might be caused by the varied types of hate speech and abusive behaviour emerged from the sample.

To start with, as mentioned in the previous section, the sample of studies reveals that the varied types of hate speech might also show some degree of overlapping on what concerns the discriminatory and intolerant ideologies fuelling them.

In this sense, it is possible to observe that studies such as Pérez Díaz and Aguilar Pérez (2021) demonstrates that xenophobic discourses on Mexican social media are also permeated with racism. In the case of politically motivated hate speech, Torbisco Cervantes and Gomero Correa (2021) reveal that in Peru, the discourses were also permeated with elements of racial discrimination. In Brazil, Silva and Aléssio (2019) reveal that homophobic hate speech is oftentimes permeated with elements of reinforcement of masculinity values, what is also found in revenge porn, as investigated in Italy by Gattamelata (2022).

**Figure 7.1**: Explanatory model of the societal impacts of social media platforms

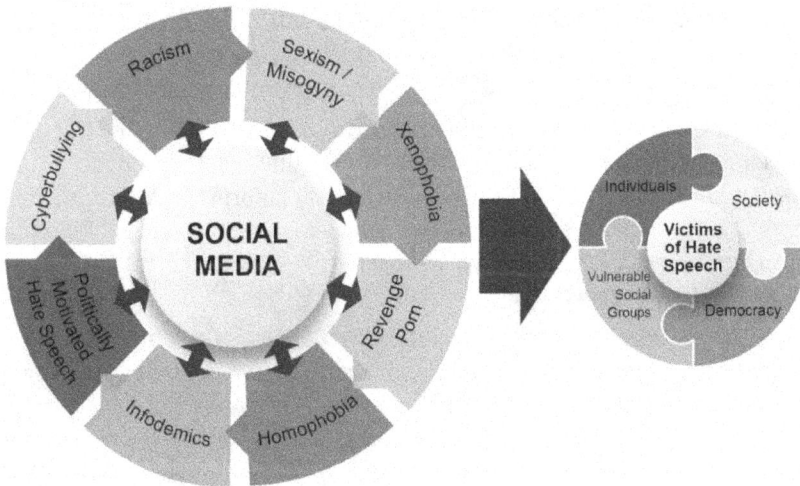

Source: the author.

Thus, it is possible to bring several other similar examples like the ones above. However, what is more important is that this reflection allows us to infer that the varied types of hate speech and abuse emerged from the sample of studies are also intertwined, and their combination can bring adverse societal impacts to different social agents and the society as well.

Then, following this line of reasoning, it has been possible to develop an explanatory model (see Figure 7.1) that integrates the main elements involved in the phenomenon of hate speech and abusive behaviour and its societal impacts.

As displayed in the explanatory model, social media platforms are at the core of manifestations of hate speech and abusive behaviour, because the technology plays the pivotal role of vehicle for the wide and instantaneous dissemination of this kind of content.

Although social media has not created or inaugurated hate speech in society, it becomes clear that this disruptive digital technology's powerful networking capabilities play a decisive role in its spread. Through social media, offenders can connect with and entice multiple like-minded people and instantaneously spread and amplify their hateful voices and intolerance at a pace and reach not previously seen in human history. Indeed, as discussed in Chapter 2, this dynamic creates echo chambers of hate.

Consequently, as a central spot where this large array of varied types of hate speech and abusive behaviour converges, it becomes clearer why social media platforms encompass a subject of concern since they play the dual role of catalyst and vehicle. They are catalysts because people who nurture and engage in hateful and discriminatory ideologies explore this digital technology to unleash their sentiments and attract multiple like-minded users. They are vehicles because their powerful networking capabilities allow users to spread hateful discourses and intolerance practically everywhere without restrictions.

Moreover, another worrisome aspect of this dynamic comprises the fact that, as addressed by different authors (Aziz, 2020; BHRRC, 2020; Trindade, 2022), the large corporations behind major social media platforms profit from hateful discourses. These authors explain that aggressive and hateful content published on social media often tends to trigger high levels of engagement (i.e., likes, comments, shares, retweets, etc.).

Besides, according to a study conducted by Trindade (2020b), this type of content tends to keep attracting new and recurring users for up to three years after the original publication of the post, which the author has coined as *the long tail of hate speech*. On top of that, taking into account that people spend several hours per day connected to social media (see Tables 4.1, 5.1, and 6.1), it means that they are prone to be exposed to many advertisements and, consequently, the corporations profit from this dynamic and feel less compelled in breaking this pernicious cycle.

Thus, obviously, the corporations do not openly and publicly endorse the dissemination of hate speech and intolerance circulating on their platforms. However, even so, they end up profiting from them, and several voices advocate that corporations usually resist effectively blocking and removing distressful content from their platforms since such measures could hinder their revenue (Aziz, 2020; BHRRC, 2020; Trindade, 2022).

Then, unpacking the victim's component in the dynamic mentioned above and displayed in the explanatory model (Figure 7.1), it is possible to notice that it encompasses four elements: 1) individuals, 2) vulnerable social groups, 3) democracy, and 4) society.

Regarding **individual victims**, there are several circumstances where offenders direct their hate and intolerance towards specific individuals, even if, with this approach, they also aim to indirectly disqualify a social group such as women, Black people, the LGBTQI+ community, and so forth. This reflection coalesces with the argument advocated by Chetty and Alathur (2018), in the sense that hate speech can negatively impact people directly or indirectly. According to the authors, in the circumstance of the direct impact of hate speech, the victims are hurt immediately by the content of hateful discourses, while in the case of the indirect impact of hate speech, the harm might eventually be delayed, meaning that the harm is perpetrated by other social agents, and not necessarily by the original aggressor. For instance, a racist hate speech manifested on social media might motivate other racists to initiate harassment, intimidation, and even engage in acts of physical violence in the offline context.

Within this context, it can be mentioned, for example, the cases of aggressive misogynistic hate speech against Brazil's former president Dilma Rousseff (Stocker and Dalmaso, 2016), the former Rio de Janeiro city councillor Marielle Franco (Silveira-Barbosa and Rocha, 2018) and a prominent Black female journalist (Rebs and Ernst, 2017), as previously analysed in Chapter 4. The verbal aggressions fostered on social media were targeted at specific persons, but in the end, the hateful discourses also included women and Black people more broadly.

What concerns **vulnerable social groups** they can encompass women, immigrants, ethnic minorities, the LGBTQI+ community, members of indigenous communities, and followers of non-Christian faiths, among others. In the sample of studies analysed in the present book, there are several supporting examples. Among them, it can be highlighted the discriminatory discourses against residents of *Aguablanca* district in Cali, who were portrayed as the contaminating vector of COVID-19 in Colombia (Arana Castañeda, 2020), the xenophobic manifestations against Nicaraguan's pupils in Costa Rica, as discussed in Chapter 5, and also against North African immigrants in Italy (Zannoni, 2017) as analysed in Chapter 6.

In general terms, from the perspective of offenders, the aforementioned vulnerable social groups have embodied the personification of 'undesirable' people, triggering some degree of discomfort in members of the hegemonic social group and becoming the target of hate speech on social media. Furthermore, in the case of abusive behaviour, such as revenge porn, oftentimes women are the predominant victims (Spallaccia, 2018; Abbatecola, 2021; Gattamelata, 2022), while cyberbullying tends to impact young people (Cera, 2017; Rega and Lovari, 2019).

Along these lines, it is possible to observe that **democratic regimes** can also be severely impacted by the spread of fake news and politically motivated hate speech that challenges, undermines, and discredits politicians and democratic institutions such as the parliament, elected officials, and the legal system. In this regard, it calls attention, for example, the racist discourses fostered on Facebook by a Peruvian congresswoman against the country's former prime minister upon his appointment as OAS representative (Torbisco Cervantes and Gomero Correa, 2021), as analysed in Chapter 5.

Additionally, amidst the challenging scenario brought by the COVID-19 pandemic, Caliandro *et al.* (2020) have addressed the issue of infodemics, which is basically made up of disinformation and unsubstantiated arguments spread rapidly through the internet and social media. As discussed in Chapter 6, this phenomenon can represent a direct threat to the public health system, and a possible ripple effect could be the indirect undermining of public trust in governmental institutions.

Then, what can also be observed comprises the fact that the recent emergence of far-right political figures to the central stage has triggered the worrisome phenomenon of ferociously depicting and treating political opponents as enemies rather than mere adversaries advocating diverse political ideologies.

Furthermore, it is imperative to say that this atmosphere fostered by politically motivated hate speech can instil people to engage in physical attacks and riots against democratic institutions. In this sense, two emblematic examples comprise the violent riots that occurred in January 2021 in the US and in Brazil in January 2023, as widely addressed by the international press (Barry *et al.*, 2021; BBC, 2021; Nicas and Spigariol, 2023; Philips and Downie, 2023). They represent the ultimate symbols of the practical effects of prolonged and consistent construction and dissemination of politically motivated hate speech, fake news and intolerance, enticing ordinary citizens to engage in hate crime.

Then, it is also possible to notice that the combination of the aforementioned societal impacts brings a ripple effect upon the overall **social fabric**. Bearing in mind that the more hate speech and abusive behaviour become naturalised or a common component of the social media landscape, the tendency is the increasing erosion of harmonious conviviality and, ultimately, the undermining of social cohesion, as argued by Bliuc *et al.* (2018). The authors argue that hate speech undermines social cohesion, since this practice is likely to create and exacerbate division in the social fabric, where multiple ethnic and racial groups co-exist.

On top of that, it cannot be disregarded the fact that contrary to what many offenders tend to believe and usually claim, the societal impacts of hate speech and abuse on social media are not restricted to the online environment. They can not only cause multiple real impacts in people's lives (e.g., depression, anxiety, low self-esteem, suicidal thoughts, panic crises, episodes of self-harm, etc.), but, in several circumstances, they can also lead to acts of physical violence and hate crimes, as already revealed in the literature (Karamanidou, 2016; Lazaridis and Veikou, 2017; Mantovan, 2018; Rzepnikowska, 2018; Virdee and McGeever, 2018).

Therefore, the combination of all these elements makes the lives of the victims extremely challenging. Within it, the individual victims, vulnerable social groups, society and even democratic regimes are affected by this spiral of hate and abuse.

Consequently, in this context, what is observed is that the 'other' or 'different' is assigned a series of negative attributes by members of hegemonic social groups in such a way that if they are not one of 'us', then they represent a 'threat', embodying the 'enemy hat' and, in this condition, they must be challenged, disqualified, devaluated and ultimately, even eliminated.

Therefore, although in several circumstances, offenders might engage in certain specific types of manifestations of hate and abuse (e.g., racism, xenophobia, misogyny, homophobia, etc.), often they overlap and bring elements of other forms of bigotry. Given the powerful networking capabilities afforded by social media platforms (not to mention the profit generated for the corporations) it means that such messages are amplified, reaching a large audience of like-minded people. Ultimately, as discussed in the present chapter and supported by the dozens of studies analysed, this pernicious dynamic represents a heavy burden to society.

## The role played by social media users

As addressed in this chapter, the examination of the sample of studies has revealed a series of main themes explored by researchers across 11 countries, which are linked, for instance, with colonial-like racist ideologies, white supremacy, the desire to reinforce one's masculinity, far-right ideas of moral superiority, and so forth.

Since in most face-to-face social interactions it is inappropriate (and in some cases even illegal) to openly manifest these types of ideologies, the literature reveals that many people who nurture them have moved to social media to unleash hateful and discriminatory ideas, as discussed in Chapter 2, and particularly supported by the works conducted by Picca and Feagin (2007), Pérez (2017) and Eschmann (2023).

Then, again resorting to the topics addressed in Chapter 2, it becomes even clearer why colour blindness is rather a myth than a reality, as argued by authors such as Daniels (2012; 2015), Kettrey and Laster (2014) and Yoon (2016), taking into account that the large array of discriminatory and intolerant ideologies emerged from the sample of studies confirm this claim. Besides, other behavioural aspects, such as the belief in online anonymity as a sort of protective shield preventing users to be held accountable for their attitudes contribute to explain belligerent behaviour online against individuals and vulnerable social groups. Furthermore, the convenient claim of right to freedom of expression is often employed by offenders to justify their aggressiveness and, as such, direct their discourse unrestricted against anyone and even challenge the integrity of democratic institutions (Quadrado and Ferreira, 2020; Torbisco Cervantes and Gomero Correa, 2021; Parodi *et al.*, 2022).

Consequently, as seen in the previous section, social media plays the pivotal role of catalyst and vehicle of hate speech, and the latter is directly influenced by users' antisocial behaviour as addressed in Chapter 2. That is, they weaponise the digital technology to serve their purpose of distilling hate and intolerance. In this sense, it is possible to observe that Casaes and Córdova (2019) argue that the internet ecosystem, especially social media, has been used to spread disinformation and foster hate and prejudice against minority and marginalised groups, a role that used to be performed by traditional institutions, such as the mass media. This practice is playing a crucial role in developing and reinforcing a series of negative social representations of Blacks, indigenous peoples, members of LGBTQ+ communities, and women, depicting them in ways that creates divisionism and prejudice.

In essence, the combination of users' antisocial behaviour can be summarised in alignment with the argumentation advocated by Pérez (2017) and Eschmann (2023), in the sense that they use or explore social media as their channel to convey and disseminate ideologies that are considered inappropriate to be openly manifested in public. Ultimately, resorting to Picca and Feagin's (2007) and Goffman's (1959) conceptualisation discussed in Chapter 2, it means to say that offenders explore social media as their 'digital backstage', since they tend to believe in the power of online anonymity and thus, as a consequence, social media allows them to hide their 'true face' from public scrutiny.

Furthermore, this scenario resonates with the words of the medical doctor Andi Nganso in an interview on La7 a few years ago[1]. When asked if he thought Italy is a racist country, he replied: "I do not think Italy is a racist country. What I believe is that racist people find a megaphone to spread their voice". So, in this sense, social media plays exactly the role of a powerful megaphone (or the vehicle, as explained in the present study).

---

[1] La7 is an Italian TV Channel and Dr Andi Nganso was the victim of an episode of racism in August 2022 in an Italian hospital where he works, when a patient refused to be touched by a Black health professional claiming that "he would infect her" (Available at: https://www.today.it/cronaca/medico-aggredito-paziente-razzista.html).

# Concluding thoughts

*"If you can only be tall because someone else is on their*
*knees, then you have a serious problem".*

(Toni Morrison)

As seen in the present study, with the emergence and proliferation of social media platforms within the past two decades, while it has transformed considerably the digital landscape and the way people communicate, it has also become a breeding ground for the manifestation and dissemination of varied types of online harassment and abuse.

Among these manifestations of intolerance, they range from racist discourses targeting marginalised communities to varied forms of hate speech, aggressive misogynistic content, revenge porn, cyberbullying, and the dissemination of misleading information. Besides, these pernicious manifestations disregard any notion of geographical boundaries, and as such, they have become a subject matter of global concern and debate.

Along these lines, and as previously explained in the Introduction chapter, the main objective of the present study was to delve into the multifaceted aspects of the phenomenon of online harassment and abuse while adopting an innovative cross-cultural approach encompassing studies published in 11 countries. This way, the present work sheds light on the intricate interplay among digital technology, varied types of online harassment and abuse, and their adverse societal impacts.

Additionally, taking into account that most of the studies in the discipline of critical social media and internet studies address Anglophone social contexts (notably the US and the UK), by adopting a cross-cultural perspective and exploring research primarily published in Italian, Portuguese, and Spanish, this work unveiled nuanced cultural and linguistic factors shaping the manifestation and adverse societal impacts of hate speech on social media. As a consequence, the study contributes to filling the existing gap regarding predominantly studied Anglophone social contexts, while the rich body of literature produced in non-hegemonic languages is often overlooked.

In this sense, Bamberg et al. (2022) criticise the hegemony of studies conducted in Anglophone contexts, arguing that the economic and technological dominance exercised by these countries results in the coloniality of knowledge and the internalisation of the higher academic relevance of their studies and also the superiority of English as a scientific language. Besides, as argued by Matamoros-Fernandez (2020, p. 6), "an understanding of the cultural specificities of harmful speech in different regions of the world is fundamental to guaranteeing that platform governance and norms are aligned with basic human rights".

To this end, the study has begun with an account of the evolution of social media and the internet, followed by the analysis of users' antisocial behavioural aspects, which have contributed to understanding why they can turn social media into a toxic virtual environment. In this sense, the study has addressed four main elements: 1) the concept of colour blindness, 2) the fallacy of online anonymity, 3) the echo chamber of hate, and 4) hate speech *vs* freedom of expression. In complement to this analysis, in the same chapter, the study has resorted to the works of Goffman (1959), Picca and Feagin (2007), Pérez (2017) and Eschmann (2023) to explain that offenders' antisocial behaviour turns social media into a toxic environment by weaponising the technology and using them as a sort of 'digital backstage' to hide their true face from public scrutiny.

Subsequently, the comprehensive analysis of a considerable number of studies has revealed the predominance of an array of themes according to the language in which they were published. In the case of studies published in Portuguese, they comprised: a) the intersection of gender, race and class, b) politically motivated hate speech, c) homophobic hate speech, and d) social representation and xenophobic discourses. Concerning studies published in Spanish, the main themes that emerged from the sample of papers were: a) xenophobic discourses, b) politically motivated hate speech, and c) deep-rooted and enduring racism. Finally, regarding studies published in Italian, the main themes comprised: a) the interplay between COVID-19 and infodemics, b) hate speech and resistance, c) xenophobia and cyberbullying, and d) revenge porn and gendered hate speech.

These chapters culminate in the development of a proposed explanatory model, which illustrates how social media plays the pivotal dual role of catalyst and vehicle for various societal issues, affecting individuals, vulnerable social groups, society, and even democracy.

Within it, while acknowledging that hate speech and abusive behaviour existed before the digital era, it is evident that social media have expanded and exacerbated this phenomenon. Besides, their exponential growth rate in number of monthly active users (as well as in revenue) has been followed by the amplification of damaging discourses. Ultimately, users' antisocial behaviour channelled through social media completes the dynamic that causes serious adverse societal impacts. Thus, it becomes clear that initiatives towards tackling the phenomenon of hate speech and abusive behaviour must be implemented at multiple levels and angles.

Therefore, while it is important to improve and update the rule of law to be in closer alignment with these new phenomena, it is also relevant that civil society and governmental institutions demand more effective actions from large corporations to reduce and eliminate hate from their platforms. In other words, they should stop playing the dual role of catalyst and vehicle of hate. Along this line, it is also possible to notice the increasing debates concerning the pressing need to regulate social media platforms (Trindade, 2023).

Furthermore, it is necessary to encourage and implement different educational measures and public awareness campaigns to deconstruct ingrained intolerant ideologies, foster more inclusive mindset and eliminate the perception that the online environment represents some sort of nobody's land, and that there are no consequences for people's attitudes. This fallacy must be challenged and exposed. As a matter of fact, social media users in general, and offenders in particular, must understand that online and offline environments are not two separate realms but rather intertwined. Thus, behaviour and attitudes fostered on social media do have consequences in people's lives outside of that environment.

Then, a final thought goes for suggestions for future studies. As already indicated in the chapters addressing the studies published in Portuguese, Spanish and Italian, social media platforms such as Instagram, Telegram, YouTube, and WhatsApp are still underexplored and deserve close attention. It is also true that, eventually, there might be some degree of methodological challenges to overcome. However, even so, they remain prolific resources for numerous social science research (qualitative, quantitative, and mixed methods). Besides, the emergence of new platforms like Meta's Threads, which competes directly with Twitter, and Discord, whose name already raises some eyebrows, might also represent potential arenas for studies.

Additionally, future studies could also explore the societal impacts of bots (or automated interactions on the internet and social media but managed by individuals or groups of individuals with specific malicious intentions) and the deep fake technology, which can manipulate voice and video images to make real people (both celebrities and ordinary citizens) to say or do things online that in real life they have not done or said. Thus, the potential to masquerade, manipulate and distort truth with this technology is enormous, worrisome, and deserves the attention of social scientists. Finally, the recent emergence of powerful Artificial Intelligence tools such as ChatGPT, Google's Bard, and their competitors might represent a whole new avenue for innovative social research.

# References

Abbatecola, E. (2021) Revenge Porn o D.I.V.I.S.E? Proposta per cambiare un'etichetta sessista, [Revenge Porn or D.I.V.I.S.E? Proposal to change a sexist label], *Incursioni: International Journal of Gender Studies*, 10 (19), 401-413.

Allcott, H. and Gentzkow, M. (2017) Social Media and Fake News in the 2016 Election, *Journal of Economic Perspectives*, 31 (2), 211-236.

Altamirano, G.F. and Torres-Toukoumidis, Á. (2021) Análisis del discurso xenófobo hacia la migración venezolana en los comentarios de las publicaciones de Facebook pertenecientes a los diarios locales, [Analysis of the xenophobic discourse towards Venezuelan migration in the comments of Facebook posts belonging to local newspapers], *GIGAPP Estudios Working Papers*, 8 (211), 310-325.

Alves, C.J.L. and Paulo, T.V. (2017) As trincheiras da fala: discurso de ódio no Facebook, [The trenches of speech: hate speech on Facebook], *Temática* 13 (4), 35-51.

Amnesty (2017) Amnesty reveals alarming impact of online abuse against women, *Amnesty International*, 20 November, New York, NY. Available from: https://www.amnesty.org/en/latest/news/2017/11/amnesty-reveals-alarming-impact-of-online-abuse-against-women/

Anjos, J.C.V. (2022) "As garras do feminismo": discurso de ódio antifeminista no Facebook e o senso de urgência controlada, ["The Claws of Feminism": Antifeminist Facebook Hate Speech and the Controlled Sense of Urgency], *Revista Brasileira de Ciências da Comunicação*, 45 (e2022119), 1-19.

Antelman, K. (2004) Do Open-Access Articles Have a Greater Research Impact? *College & Research Libraries*, 65 (5), 372-382.

AP (2020) Explaining AP style on Black and white, *The Associated Press*, 20 July, New York, NY. Available from: https://apnews.com/article/9105661462

Apuke, O.D. and Omar, B. (2021) Fake news and COVID-19: modelling the predictors of fake news sharing among social media users, *Telematics and Informatics*, 56.

Arana Castañeda, C. (2020) "El oriente de Cali no tiene ni Dios ni ley": redes sociales digitales y violencia racializada a propósito de la COVID-19, ["The east of Cali has neither God nor law": digital social media and racialized violence purpose of COVID-19], *Summa*, 2, 217-243.

Arcila Calderón, C., Blanco-Herrero, D. and Valdez-Apolo, M.B. (2020) Rechazo y discurso de odio en Twitter: análisis de contenido de los tuits sobre migrantes y refugiados en español, [Rejection and Hate Speech in Twitter: Content Analysis of Tweets about Migrants and Refugees in Spanish], *Revista Española de Investigaciones Sociológicas*, (172), 21-40.

Arévalo, A. and Duarte, H. (2018) De lo hardcore a lo lightInjurias y homofobia cordial en El Salvador, [From the hardcore to the lightInsults and cordial homophobia in El Salvador], *Civitas: Revista de Ciências Sociais*, 18 (1), 43-64.

Arriaga Arango, E. (2013) Racismo y discurso en la era digital: el caso de la revista Hola y los discursos en las redes sociales, [Racism and discourse in the digital era: the case of Hola Magazine and the discourses in social networks], *Discurso & Sociedad*, 7 (4), 617-642.

Awan, I. (2016) Islamophobia on Social Media: A Qualitative Analysis of the Facebook's Walls of Hate, *International Journal of Cyber Criminology*, 10 (1), 1-20.

Azevedo, J.C., Miranda, F.A. and Souza, C.H.M. (2012) Reflexões a cerca das estruturas psíquicas e a prática do Ciberbullying no contexto da escola, [Reflections about the psychic structures and practice in the school context Ciberbullying], *Revista Brasileira de Ciências da Comunicação*, 35 (2), 247-265.

Azevedo, M.M. (2008) Diagnóstico da população indígena no Brasil, [Diagnosis of the indigenous population in Brazil], *Ciência e Cultura (SBPC)*, 60 (4), 19-22.

Aziz, A. (2020) Facebook Ad Boycott Campaign 'Stop Hate For Profit' Gathers Momentum And Scale: Inside The Movement For Change, *Forbes*, 24 June, New York, NY. Available from: https://www.forbes.com/sites/afdhelaziz/2020/06/24/facebook-ad-boycott-campaign-stop-hate-for-profit-gathers-momentum-and-scale-inside-the-movement-for-change/?sh=62b473116687

Bagua, A.M. (2020) Representación del indígena en Twitter. Caso: Mushuc Runa Sporting Club, [Indigenous representation on Twitter. Case: Mushuc Runa Sporting Club], *Revista Estudios de la Gestión*, (7), 197-224.

Bamberg, C.R.F.P.A., Vital, L.P., Costa, A. and Garcez, D.C. (2022) Epistemologia Decolonial e Ciência da Informação: uma análise dos anais do ENANCIB, [Decolonial Epistemology and Information Science: ananalysis of ENANCIB Annals], *InCID: Revista de Ciência da Informação e Documentação*, 13 (2), 29-46.

Barreto Junior, I.F. (2022) *Fake News: Anatomia da desinformação, discurso de ódio e erosão da democracia*, [Fake News: Anatomy of Disinformation, Hate Speech and the Erosion of Democracy]. São Paulo, SP: Saraiva Expressa Jur.

Barry, D., McIntire, M. and Rosenberg, M. (2021) "'Our President Wants Us Here': The Mob That Stormed the Capitol", *The New York Times*, 09 January, New York, NY. Available from: https://www.nytimes.com/2021/01/09/us/capitol-rioters.html

Bastos, G.G., Garcia, D.A. and Sousa, L.M.A. (2017) A homofobia em discurso: Direitos Humanos em circulação, [A homofobia em discurso: Direitos Humanos em circulação], *Linguagem em (Dis)curso*, 17 (1), 11-24.

Bates, S. (2016) Revenge Porn and Mental Health: A Qualitative Analysis of the Mental Health Effects of Revenge Porn on Female Survivors, *Feminist Criminology*, 12 (1), 22-42.

BBC (2013) Yahoo to shut down pioneering AltaVista search site, *BBC News*, 01 July, London, UK. Available from: https://www.bbc.com/news/technology-23127361

BBC (2021) Capitol riots timeline: What happened on 6 January 2021? *BBC News*, London, UK. Available from: https://www.bbc.com/news/world-us-canada-56004916

Benevides, B.G. (2023) *Dossiê: Assassinatos e violências contra travestis e transexuais brasileiras em 2022*, [Dossier: Murders and violence against Brazilian transvestites and transsexuals in 2022]. Brasília, DF: ANTRA - Associação Nacional de Travestis e Transexuais

Bentivegna, S. and Rega, R. (2020) I discorsi d'odio online in una prospettiva comunicativa: un'agenda per la ricercar, [Online hate speech in a communicative perspective: an agenda for research], *Mediascapes Journal*, (16), 151-171.

Bertoni, S. (2011) Sean Parker: Agent Of Disruption, *Forbes*, 21 September, New York, NY. Available from: https://www.forbes.com/sites/stevenbertoni/2011/09/21/sean-parker-agent-of-disruption/?sh=433feae07000

Bhasin, H. (2019) The History Of Search Engines (Complete Timeline from Starting), *Marketing 91*, 08 July, Maharashtra, India. Available from: https://www.marketing91.com/history-of-search-engines/

BHRRC (2020) More than 500 companies join Facebook ad boycott 'stop hate for profit', *Business & Human Rights Resource Centre*, 01 July, London, UK. Available from: https://www.business-humanrights.org/en/latest-news/more-than-500-companies-join-facebook-ad-boycott-stop-hate-for-profit/

Bliuc, A.-M., Faulkner, N., Jakubowicz, A. and McGarty, C. (2018) Online networks of racial hate: A systematic review of 10 years of research on cyber-racism, *Computers in Human Behavior*, (87), 75-86.

Bonfils, M. (2011) Why Facebook is Wiping Out Orkut in India & Brazil, *Search Engine Watch*, 13 April, London, UK. Available from: http://searchenginewatch.com/sew/opinion/2064470/why-facebook-wiping-out-orkut-india-brazil

Borges, R.C.S. and Melo, G.C.V. (2019) Quando a raça e o gênero estão em questão: embates discursivos em rede social, [When Race and Gender are on Focus: Discursive Confrontations on Social Network], *Revista Estudos Feministas*, 27 (2), 1-13.

Bortone, R. and Cerquozzi, F. (2017) L'hate speech al tempo di Internet, [Hate speech in internet times], *Aggiornamenti Sociali*, (Dicembre), 818-827.

Boxman-Shabtai, L. and Shifman, L. (2015) When ethnic humor goes digital, *New Media & Society*, 17 (4), 520-539.

boyd, d.m. (2015) Social Media: A Phenomenon to be Analyzed, *Social Media + Society*, 1 (1), 1-2.

Bustos Martínez, L., De Santiago Ortega, P.P., Martinez Miró, M.Á. and Rengifo Hidalgo, M.S. (2019) Discursos de odio: una epidemia que se propaga en la red. Estado de la cuestión sobre el racismo y la xenofobia en las redes sociales, [Hate speech: an epidemic spreading in the network. State of the art on racism and xenophobia on social media], *Mediaciones Sociales*, 18, 25-42.

Caers, R., De Feyter, T., De Couck, M., Stough, T., Vigna, C. and Du Bois, C. (2013) Facebook: A literature review, *New Media & Society*, 15 (6), 982-1002.

Caliandro, A., Anselmi, G. and Sturiale, V. (2020) Fake news, Covid-19 e Infodemia: un esempio di ricerca sociale in real-time su Twitter, [Fake news, Covid-19 and Infodemia: an example of real-time social research on Twitter], *Mediascapes Journal*, (15), 174-188.

Campillo Muñoz, S. (2019) Propuesta de clasificación de actos verbales violentos en las redes sociales, *E-Aesla*, (5), 199-207.

Cann, A., Dimitriou, K. and Hooley, T. (2011) Social Media: A guide for researchers, *Research Information Network*, February, Leicster, UK, 48 pages. Available from: http://www.rin.ac.uk/social-media-guide

Carrillo Urcid, E. (2020) Discurso racista mexicano en redes sociales, [Mexican racist discourse in social network], *Signos Lingüísticos*, 16 (32), 50-81.

Carvalho, F.C., Massuchin, M.G. and Mitozo, I.B. (2018) Radicalização nas redes sociais: comentários no Facebook durante a disputa presidencial em 2014 no Brasil, [Radicalização nas redes sociais: comentários no Facebook durante a disputa presidencial em 2014 no Brasil], *Análise Social*, (229), 898-926.

Casaes, D. and Córdova, Y. (2019) Weaponised Information in Brazil: Digitising Hate, *Toda Peace Institute*, November, Tokyo, Japan, 1-18. Available from: https://toda.org/policy-briefs-and-resources/policy-briefs/weaponised-information-in-brazil-digitising-hate.html

Castells, M. (2010) The Information Technology Revolution, IN: Castells, M. (ed.) *The Rise of the Network Society*. New York, NY: Wiley-Blackwell, 28-76.

Castro, A. (2018) Google turns 20: how an internet search engine reshaped the world, *The Verge*, 27 September, New York, NY. Available from: https://www.theverge.com/2018/9/5/17823490/google-20th-birthday-anniversary-history-milestones

Castro Martínez, A. and Díaz Morilla, P. (2021) La comunicación política de la derecha radical en redes sociales. De Instagram a TikTok y Gab, la estrategia digital de Vox, [The political communication of the radical right in social networks. From Instagram to TikTok and Gab, Vox's digital strategy], *Dígitos: Revista de Comunicación Digital*, (7), 67-89.

Cera, R. (2017) Social network, scuole e famiglie: una revisione della letteratura scientifica, [Social networks, schools and families: a review of the scientific literature], *Annali Online della Didattica e della Formazione Docente*, 9 (13), 164-194.

Cerna Aragón, D. (2017) ¿Quién es el troll?: La construcción de identidades políticas en social media en el contexto peruano, [Who is the Troll?: The Construction of Political Identities on Social Media in the Peruvian Context], *Contratexto: revista de la Facultad de Comunicación de la Universidad de Lima*, (28), 71-92.

Chadwick, J. (2023) Meta's Threads app GOES LIVE: Mark Zuckerberg launches 'Twitter-killer' app where users can share text, links, photos and videos, *Daily Mail*, 06 July, London, UK. Available from: https://www.dailymail.co.uk/sciencetech/article-12266877/Mark-Zuckerbergs-Meta-officially-launches-Twitter-rival-Threads.html

Chandra, R. (2020) Calling COVID-19 a "Chinese Virus" or "Kung Flu" Is Racist, *Psychology Today*, 18 March, New York, NY. Available from: https://www.psychologytoday.com/us/blog/the-pacific-heart/202003/calling-covid-19-chinese-virus-or-kung-flu-is-racist

Chaudhry, I. and Gruzd, A. (2019) Expressing and challenging racist discourses on Facebook: how social media weaken the "Spiral of Silence" Theory, *Policy and Internet*, 12 (1), 88-108.

Chetty, N. and Alathur, S. (2018) Hate speech review in the context of online social networks, *Aggression and Violent Behavior*, 40, 108-118.

Cogburn, D.L. and Espinoza-Vasquez, F.K. (2011) From Networked Nominee to Networked Nation: Examining the Impact of Web 2.0 and Social Media on Political Participation and Civic Engagement in the 2008 Obama Campaign, *Journal of Political Marketing*, 10 (1-2), 189-213.

Coleman, N. (2020) Why We're Capitalizing Black, *The New York Times*, 5 July, New York, NY. Available from: https://www.nytimes.com/2020/07/05/insider/capitalized-black.html

Cologna, D.B. (2020) Le tentazioni sinofobiche italiane dopo un anno di pandemia globale, [Italian Sinophobic temptations after a year of global pandemic], *Orizzonte Cina*, 11 (3), 76-80.

Conger, K. and Hirsch, L. (2022) Elon Musk Completes $44 Billion Deal to Own Twitter, *The New York Times*, 27 October, New York, NY. Available from: https://www.nytimes.com/2022/10/27/technology/elon-musk-twitter-deal-complete.html

Costa, A.M. (2017) "Mal Amadas", "Porcas", "Feminazis", "Sujas", "Xanatunzel", "Nojentas" e "Xontuzeis" – Análise dos Discursos de Ódio sobre a performance Pelos Pêlos e seus desdobramentos, ["Mal Amadas", "Porcas", "Feminazis", "Sujas", "Xanatunzel", "Nojentas" and "Xontuzeis" - Analysis of Hate Speeches about the Pelosi performance and its consequences], *Revista de Estudos Interdisciplinares em Gêneros e Sexualidades*, 1 (7), 157-178.

Costa, P.R. (2020) Uma cartografia do ódio no Facebook: gatilhos, insultos e imitações, [A map of hate on Facebook: triggers, insults and imitations], *Comunicação Pública*, 15 (29), 1-27.

Crystal, D. (2003) *English as a global language*, 2nd ed. Cambridge, UK: Cambridge University Press

D'Ancona, M.Á.C. (2018) What determines the rejection of immigrants through an integrative model, *Social Science Research*, (74), 1-15.

Daniels, J. (2009) *Cyber Racism: White Supremacy Online and the New Attack on Civil Rights*. Lanham, Maryland: Rowan & Littlefield Publishers, Inc.

Daniels, J. (2012) Race and racism in Internet Studies: A review and critique, *New Media & Society*, 15 (5), 695-719.

Daniels, J. (2015) "My Brain Database Doesn't See Skin Color": Color-Blind Racism in the Technology Industry and in Theorizing the Web, *American Behavioral Scientist*, 59 (11), 1377-1393.

Delacourt, J.T. (1997) The international impact of internet regulation, *Harvard International Law Journal*, 38 (1), 207-235.

Deligiannis, N., Do Huu, T., Nguyen, D.M. and Luo, X. (2018) Deep Learning for Geolocating Social Media Users and Detecting Fake News, *NATO STO Meetings Proceedings*, 1-12.

Desjardins, J. (2016) Chart: The Rise and Fall of Yahoo, *Visual Capitalist*, 29 July, New York, NY. Available from: https://www.visualcapitalist.com/chart-rise-fall-yahoo/

Di Fátima, B., Gouveia, C. and Lapa, T. (2020) Porto *vs* Benfica. Uma cartografia entre o amor e o ódio no Twitter, [Porto *vs* Benfica. A cartography between love and hate on Twitter], *Estudos em Comunicação*, (30), 147-175.

Dinucci, D. (1999) Fragmented Future, *Print Magazine*, 54 (3), 32;221-222.

Dunham, J. (2016) *Freedom of the press 2016*, Washington, D.C., Freedom House. Available from: https://freedomhouse.org/sites/default/files/FH_FTOP_2016Report_Final_04232016.pdf

EC (2022) Horizon Europe: Programme Guide, *Euroean Commision*, 12 April, Brussels, Belgium. Available from: https://ec.europa.eu/info/funding-tenders/opportunities/docs/2021-2027/horizon/guidance/programme-guide_horizon_en.pdf

ECRI (2018) Racist and xenophobic hate speech on the rise despite considerable preventive efforts, *European Commission against Racism and Intolerance*, 27 February, Stockholm, Sweden. Available from: http://hudoc.ecri.coe.int/eng?i=SWE-PR-V-2018-263-ENG

ECRI (2019) *Annual Report of ECRI's Activities.* Strasbourg, France: ECRI - European Commission against Racism and Intolerance

ECRI (2020) ECRI annual report: Racism, racial discrimination, xenophobia, anti-semitism and intolerance are on the rise in Europe, *Newsroom*, 27 February, Strasbourg, France. Available from: https://www.coe.int/en/web/portal/-/ecri-annual-report-racism-racial-discrimination-xenophobia-anti-semitism-and-intolerance-are-on-the-rise-in-europe

Egelman, S., Bernd, J., Friedland, G. and Garcia, D. (2016) The Teaching Privacy Curriculum, *Proceedings of the 47th ACM Technical Symposium on Computing Science Education*, 591-596.

Erjavec, K. and Kovačič, M.P. (2012) "You Don't Understand, This is a New War!" Analysis of Hate Speech in News Web Sites' Comments, *Mass Communication and Society*, 15, 899-920.

Eschmann, R.D. (2023) *When the hood comes off: Racism and resistance in the digital age.* California, LA: University of California Press

Feitosa E Paiva, G.M. and Silva, T.M.O. (2019) Do preconceito à (im)polidez: aspectos sociais, ideológicos e linguísticos que circunscrevem práticas racistas e sexistas no Facebook, [From prejudice to (im)politeness: social, ideological and linguistic aspects that produce racist and sexist practices on Facebook], *Cadernos de Linguagem e Sociedade*, 20 (especial), 117-133.

Fernandes, S., Nascimento, M., Pereira, A., Melo, E. and Carlos, K. (2020) Relações raciais digitais: um estudo sobre as formas de expressão da intolerância racial no Facebook, [Digital race relations: a study about forms of expression of racual intolerance on Facebook], *Revista Ibérica de Sistemas e Tecnologias de Informação*, (38), 79-91.

Fernandes, S.M.C. (2003) Representações sociais e educação especial: sentidos, identidade, silenciamentos, [Social representations and special education: meanings, identity, silencing], *Benjamin Constant*, 9 (24), 14-19.

Fernández Fernández, Á., Revilla Guijarro, A. and Andaluz Antón, L. (2020) Análisis de la caracterización discursiva de los relatos migratorios en Twitter. El caso Aquarius, [Analysis of the discursive characterization of migratory stories on Twitter: The Aquarius case], *Revista Latina de Comunicación Social*, (77), 1-18.

Ferrándiz, J., Ibáñez, C. and Espinosa, A. (2011) Racismo 2.0: expresiones de prejuicio en las redes sociales virtuales tras las elecciones generales de 2011,

[Racism 2.0: expressions of prejudice in virtual social networks after the 2011 general elections], *Politai: Revista de Ciencia Política*, 2 (3), 75-83.

Fildes, J. (2008) Final goodbye for early web icon, *BBC News*, 29 February, London, UK. Available from: http://news.bbc.co.uk/2/hi/technology/7270583.stm

Finighan, A. (2023) Will 'X' mark the spot for Elon Musk and Twitter? *AlJazeera*, 24 July, London, UK. Available from: https://www.aljazeera.com/program/inside-story/2023/7/24/will-x-mark-the-spot-for-elon-musk-and-twitter

Flannery, M.R.S. (2017) "Triste realidade": Construindo solidariedade em reação à discriminação racial no Facebook, ["Sad reality": Constructing solidarity in reaction to racial discrimination on Facebook], *Revista Entrelinhas*, 11 (2), 285-300.

Forti, L.R., Solino, L.A. and Szabo, J.K. (2021) Trade-off between urgency and reduced editorial capacity affect publication speed in ecological and medical journals during 2020, *Humanities and Social Sciences Communications*, 8 (234), 1-9.

FRA (2017) *Challenges to women's human rights in the EU: Gender discrimination, sexist hate speech and gender-based violence against women and girls*. Vienna, Austria: FRA - European Union Agency for Fundamental Rights

Fuchs, C. (2008) *Internet and Society: Social Theory in the Information Age*. New York, NY: Routledge

Fumagalli, C. (2019) Discorsi d'odio come pratiche ordinarie, [Hate speech as ordinary practice], *Biblioteca della libertà, LIV*, (224), 55-75.

Gagliardone, I., Gal, D., Alves, T. and Martinez, G. (2015) *Countering Online Hate Speech*. Paris, France: UNESCO

Gandra, A. (2023) Censo registra 1.652.876 pessoas indígenas no Brasil. [Census registers 1,652,876 indigenous people in Brazil], *Agência Brasil*, 03 April, Rio de Janeiro, RJ. Available from: https://agenciabrasil.ebc.com.br/geral/noticia/2023-04/censo-registra-1652876-pessoas-indigenas-no-brasil

Gattamelata, A. (2022) Cyberbullismo e revenge porn: como l'emergenza pandemica ha amplificato nuove forme di devianza, [Cyberbullying and Revenge Porn: How the Pandemic Emergency has Amplified New Forms of Deviance], *Ricognizioni: Rivista di Lingue, Letterature e Culture Moderne*, 9 (18), 173-180.

Gaulé, P. and Maystre, N. (2011) Getting cited: Does open access help? *Research Policy*, 40 (10), 1332-1338.

Ghoshdr, P. and Chitra, C. (2014) Death of Orkut = Rise of Facebook: a new era of social networking in cyber world, *International Journal of Marketing*, 3 (9), 81-93.

Gibson, C. (1963) Colonial Institutions and Contemporary Latin America: Social and Cultural Life, *Hispanic American Historical Review*, 43, 3 (380-389).

Giglietto, F., Rossi, L. and Bennato, D. (2012) The open laboratory: Limits and possibilities of using Facebook, Twitter, and YouTube as a research data source, *Journal of Technology in Human Services*, 30 (4), 145-159.

Goffman, E. (1959) *The presentation of self in everyday life*. New York, NY: Doubleday Anchor Books

Google (2014) Adeus ao Orkut. [Farewell to Orkut], *Google Brasil*, São Paulo, SP, Available from: http://googlebrasilblog.blogspot.com.br/2014/06/adeus-ao-orkut.html

Guardian (2016) Facebook to expand 'like' feature with five new emoji options, *The Guardian*, 28 January, London, UK. Available from: http://www.theguardian.com/technology/2016/jan/28/facebook-to-expand-like-feature-with-five-new-emoji-options

Hadero, H. (2023) Mark Zuckerberg's Threads app is scooping up millions of Twitter power users - but a culture clash is brewing, *Fortune*, 11 July, New York, NY. Available from: https://fortune.com/2023/07/11/mark-zuckerberg-threads-twitter-users-culture-clash/

Halfeld, P.C. (2013) A produção do humor na rede social Facebook, [Production of humor on Facebook], *Revista Soletras*, (26), 219-236.

Hansen, M.B.N. (2006) *Bodies in Code: Interfaces with Digital Media*. New York, NY: Routledge

Henn, R., Machado, F.V.K. and Gonzatti, C. (2019) Todos nascemos nus e o resto é drag: performatividade dos corpos construídos em sites de redes sociais, [We're all born naked and the rest is drag: performativity of the bodies constructed in social media], *Intercom - Revista Brasileira de Ciências da Comunicação*, 42 (3).

Hernández-Santaolalla, V. and Sola-Morales, S. (2019) Postverdad y discurso intimidatorio en Twitter durante el referéndum catalán del 1-O, [Post-truth and intimidation on Twitter during Catalan referendum 1-O], *Observatorio*,13 (1), 102-121.

Hilgert, J.G. and Neto, A.B. (2017) A irrupção do ódio na internet: traços discursivos de sua manifestação no Facebook, [The outbreak of hate on the internet: discursive traces of its manifestation on Facebook], *Desenredo*,13 (3), 733-745.

Hong, F.C.F., Pecotich, A. and J. Shultz Ii, C. (2002) Brand Name Translation: Language Constraints, Product Attributes, and Consumer Perceptions in East and Southeast Asia, *Journal of International Marketing*, 10 (2), 29-45.

Hughes, A. (2023) ChatGPT: Everything you need to know about OpenAI's GPT-4 tool, *BBC News*, 16 March, London, UK. Available from: https://www.sciencefocus.com/future-technology/gpt-3/

Hughes, T. (2015) Country Report: Brazil's Marco Civil da Internet, *Article 19*, 5 November, London, UK. Available from: https://www.article19.org/resources.php/resource/38175/en/country-report:-brazil's-marco-civil-da-internet

Hughey, M.W. and Daniels, J. (2013) Racist comments at online news sites: a methodological dilemma for discourse analysis, *Media, Culture & Society*, 35 (3), 332-347.

Islam, K., Ntarzanou, V. and Pereira, M.P.F.A. (2014) *Standards Wars: Google vs. Altavista (Yahoo)*. Monography, Aalborg University. Information Technology

Jakubowicz, A., Dunn, K., Manson, G., Paradies, Y., Bliuc, A.-M., Bahfen, N., Oboler, A., Atie, R. and Connely, K. (2017) *Cyber Racism and Community Resilience: Strategies for Combating Online Race Hate*. Sydney, Australia: Palgrave Macmillan

Jane, E.A. (2017) *Misogyny Online: A Short (and Brutish) History*. London, UK: Sage Publications Ltd.

Jay, P. (2008) Curtains for Netscape, *CBC News*, 29 February, Vancouver, Canada. Available from: https://www.cbc.ca/technology/technology-blog/2008/02/curtains-for-netscape.html

Jenkins, J. (2013) *English as a Lingua Franca in the International University: The Politics of Academic English Language Policy*. London, UK: Routledge

Jorgensen, M. and Phillips, L.J. (2002) *Discourse analysis as theory and method*. New York, NY: Sage Publications

Justwan, F., Baumgaertner, B., Carlisle, J.E., Clark, A.K. and Clark, M. (2018) Social media echo chambers and satisfaction with democracy among Democrats and Republicans in the aftermath of the 2016 US elections, *Journal of Elections, Public Opinion and Parties*, 1-19.

Karamanidou, L. (2016) Violence against migrants in Greece: beyond the Golden Dawn, *Ethnic and Racial Studies*, 39 (11), 2002-2021.

Kelly, N. (2020) Name Your Brand with a Global Audience in Mind, *Harvard Business Review*, 10 September, Cambridge, MA. Available from: https://hbr.org/2020/09/name-your-brand-with-a-global-audience-in-mind

Kelly, S., Truong, M., Shahbaz, A. and Earp, M. (2016) *Freedom on the Net 2016*, New York, NY, Freedom House. Available from: https://freedomhouse.org/sites/default/files/FOTN_2016_BOOKLET_FINAL.pdf

Kemp, S. (2023a) Digital 2023 - Portugal, *We are Social*, 13 February, New York, NY. Available from: https://datareportal.com/reports/digital-2023-portugal

Kemp, S. (2023b) Digital 2023: Argentina, *We are Social*, 12 February, New York, NY. Available from: https://datareportal.com/reports/digital-2023-argentina

Kemp, S. (2023c) Digital 2023: Brazil, *We are Social*, 13 February, New York, NY. Available from: https://datareportal.com/reports/digital-2023-brazil

Kemp, S. (2023d) Digital 2023: Colombia, *We are Social*, 13 February, New York, NY. Available from: https://datareportal.com/reports/digital-2023-colombia

Kemp, S. (2023e) Digital 2023: Costa Rica, *We are Social*, 13 February, New York, NY. Available from: https://datareportal.com/reports/digital-2023-costa-rica

Kemp, S. (2023f) Digital 2023: El Salvador, *We are Social*, 13 February, New York, NY. Available from: https://datareportal.com/reports/digital-2023-el-salvador

Kemp, S. (2023g) Digital 2023: Equador, *We are Social*, 13 February, New York, NY. Available from: https://datareportal.com/reports/digital-2023-ecuador

Kemp, S. (2023h) Digital 2023: Global Overview Report, *We are Social*, 26 January, New York, NY. Available from: https://wearesocial.com/it/blog/2023/01/digital-2023-i-dati-globali/

Kemp, S. (2023i) Digital 2023: Italy, *We are Social*, 13 February, New York, NY. Available from: https://datareportal.com/reports/digital-2023-italy

Kemp, S. (2023j) Digital 2023: Mexico, *We are Social*, 13 February, New York, NY. Available from: https://datareportal.com/reports/digital-2023-mexico

Kemp, S. (2023k) Digital 2023: Peru, *We are Social*, 13 February, New York, NY. Available from: https://datareportal.com/reports/digital-2023-peru

Kemp, S. (2023l) Digital 2023: Spain, *We are Social*, 13 February, New York, NY. Available from: https://datareportal.com/reports/digital-2023-spain

Kettrey, H.H. and Laster, W.N. (2014) Staking Territory in the "World White Web": An Exploration of the Roles of Overt and Color-Blind Racism in Maintaining Racial Boundaries on a Popular Web Site, *Social Currents*, 1 (3), 257-274.

Kleinman, Z. (2023) Bard: Google's rival to ChatGPT launches for over-18s, *BBC News*, 22 March, London, UK. Available from: https://www.bbc.com/news/technology-65018107

Kling, R., Lee, Y.-C., Teich, A. and Frankel, M.S. (1999) Assessing Anonymous Communication on the Internet: Policy Deliberations, *The Information Society*, (15), 79-90.

Kolko, B.E., Nakamura, L. and Rodman, G.B. (2000) *Race in Cyberspace*. New York, NY: Routledge

Larsson, A.O. (2015) Comparing to Prepare: Suggesting Ways to Study Social Media Today—and Tomorrow, *Social Media + Society*, 1 (1), 1-2.

Laws, M. (2020) Why we capitalize 'Black' (and not 'white'), *Columbia Journalism Review*, 16 June, New York, NY. Available from: https://www.cjr.org/analysis/capital-b-black-styleguide.php

Lazaridis, G. and Veikou, M. (2017) The rise of the far right in Greece and opposition to 'othering', hate speech, and crime by civil and civic organizations, *Journal of Civil Society*, 13 (1), 1-17.

Lerman, R. (2022) Elon Musk bought Twitter. Now what? *The Washington Post*, 28 October, Washington, DC. Available from: https://www.washingtonpost.com/technology/2022/10/28/elon-musk-acquisition-twitter/

Lévy, P. (2001) *Cyberculture*. Saint Paul, MN: University of Minnesota Press

London, E.B. (2010) Climate, *Embassy of Brazil in London*, 6 December, London, UK. Available from: https://web.archive.org/web/20101206014542/http://www.brazil.org.uk/brazilinbrief/climate.html

Lopes, D.A. and Figueiredo, A. (2018) Educação antirracista e ciberativismo: Experiência de coletivos de mulheres negras crespas e cacheadas no Facebook e em Salvador/BA, [Antiracist education and cyberactivism: The experience of crespas and cacheadas black women's collectives on Facebook and in Salvador/BA], *Sitientibus*, (59), 15-22.

Lovari, A. and Giglietto, F. (2012) Social Media and Italian Universities: An Empirical Study on the Adoption and Use of Facebook, Twitter and Youtube, *SSRN Electronic Journal*, 1-25.

Lovari, A. and Righetti, N. (2020) La comunicazione pubblica della salute tra infodemia e fake news: il ruolo della pagina Facebook del Ministero della Salute nella sfida social al Covid-19, [Public health communication between infodemic and fake news: the role of the Ministry of Health's Facebook page in the social challenge to Covid-19], *Mediascapes Journal*, (15), 156-173.

Lucca, B. (2023) Brasil é o país que mais mata transexuais e travestis pelo 14º ano seguido. [Brazil is the country that most kills transsexuals and transvestites for the 14th year in a row], *Folha de S. Paulo*, 26 January, São Paulo, SP. Available from: https://www1.folha.uol.com.br/cotidiano/2023/01/brasil-e-o-pais-que-mais-mata-transexuais-e-travestis-pelo-14o-ano-seguido.shtml

Luz, L.F. (2019) Raça e representação: ecos no Facebook de um engodo racial na política, [Race and representation: Facebook's echoes of a racial deception in politics], *Extraprensa*, 12 (especial), 505-519.

Maia, R.C.M. and Rezende, T.A.S. (2015) Democracia e a ecologia complexa das redes sociais online: um estudo sobre discussões acerca do racismo e da homofobia, [Democracy and the complex ecology of online social networks: a study on discussions about racism and homophobia], *Intexto*, (34), 492-512.

Mantilla, K. (2013) Gendertrolling: Misogyny Adapts to New Media, *Feminist Studies*, 39 (2), 563-570.

Mantovan, C. (2018) 'They treat us like criminals': urban public spaces and ethnic discrimination in Italy, *Patterns of Prejudice*, 1-17.

Marta-Lazo, C., Osuna-Acedo, S. and Gil-Quintana, J. (2020) La producción del discurso escrito en redes sociales respecto a las desapariciones de personas y consiguientes juicios paralelos. Caso de Gabriel Cruz (España) en Twitter y Facebook, [The production of written discourse on social networks regarding people's disappearances and consequent parallel trials. Case of Gabriel Cruz (Spain) on Twitter and Facebook], *Revista Signos*, 53 (103), 449-467.

Martins, L.a.B. (2019) O Discurso Da Intolerância Contra A Mulher Nas Redes Sociais, [The Discourse Of Intolerance Against Women In Social Networks], *RELACult - Revista Latino-Americana de Estudos em Cultura e Sociedade*, 5 (edição espcial), 1-10.

Mascheroni, G. and Mattoni, A. (2013) Electoral campaigning 2.0: The case of Italian regional elections, *Journal of Information Technology & Politics*, 10 (2), 223-240.

Matamoros-Fernandez, A. (2020) 'El Negro de WhatsApp' meme, digital blackface, and racism on social media, *First Monday*, 25 (1), 1-16.

Matamoros-Fernandez, A. and Farkas, J. (2021) Racism, Hate Speech, and Social Media: A Systematic Review and Critique, *Television & New Media*, 22 (2), 205-224.

May, C. (2019) Academic publishing and open access: Costs, benefits and options for publishing research, *Politics*, 40 (1), 120-135.

Maynard, D.C.S. (2014) Intolerância ao Sul da América: estudo comparado de grupos fascistas do Brasil e da Argentina na Internet (1996-2007), [Intolerance South of America: Comparative study of fascist groups from Brazil and Argentina on the Internet (1996-2007)], *Tempo & Argumento*, 6 (12).

McCallum, S. (2023) Elon Musk: Twitter rebrands as X and kills off blue bird logo, *BBC News*, 25 July, London, UK. Available from: https://www.bbc.co.uk/news/business-66284304

Mejía Núñez, G. (2022) La blanquitud en México según Cosas de Whitexicans, [Whiteness in Mexico according to Cosas de Whitexicans], *Revista Mexicana de Sociología*, 84 (3), 717-751.

Meneses, D. (2019) Con Mis Hijos No Te Metas: un estudio de discurso y poder en un grupo de Facebook peruano opuesto a la "ideología de género", [Con Mis Hijos No Te Metas: a study of discourse and power in a Peruvian Facebook group opposing "gender ideology"], *Anthropologica*, 37 (42), 129-154.

Mercuri, K.T. and Lima-Lopes, R.E. (2020) Discurso de ódio em mídias sociais como estratégia de persuasão popular, [Hate speech in social media as a popular persuasion strategy], *Trab. Ling. Aplic.*, (59), 1216-1238.

Milicia, M.T. (2016) Nel laboratorio sociale dell'odio: un anno di ordinario razzismo su Facebook, [In the social laboratory of hate: a year of ordinary racism on Facebook], *VOCI*, 124-147.

Milmo, D. (2023) Zuckerberg's 'Twitter killer' Threads hits 70m sign-ups in two days, *The Guardian*, 07 July, London, UK. Available from: https://www.the guardian.com/technology/2023/jul/07/mark-zuckerberg-twitter-killer-threads-hits-sign-ups-two-days

Misoch, S. (2015) Stranger on the internet: Online self-disclosure and the role of visual anonymity, *Computers in Human Behavior*, 48, 535-541.

Moscovici, S. (1988) Notes towards a description of Social Representations, *European Journal of Social Psychology*, 18 (3), 211-250.

Moscovici, S. (1994) Social representations and pragmatic communication, *Social Science Information*, 33 (2), 163-177.

Moura, R.M.F. and Souza, M.J.M. (2019) O Venezuelano invasor em Boa Vista - RR: Uma análise crítica dos discursos de ódio no Facebook, [The Venezuelan invader in Boa Vista (RR): a critical analysis of hate discourses on Facebook], *Revista X*, 14 (6), 44-65.

Murphy, H., Aliaj, O., Fontanella-Khan, J. and Bradshaw, T. (2022) Elon Musk closes $44bn deal to buy Twitter, *Financial Times*, 28 October, London, UK. Available from: https://www.ft.com/content/b429b624-bf82-4ccd-bf69-b75 055403952

Nicas, J. and Spigariol, A. (2023) Bolsonaro Supporters Lay Siege to Brazil's Capital, *The New York Times*, 08 January, New York, NY. Available from: https://www.nytimes.com/2023/01/08/world/americas/brazil-election-protests-bolsonaro.html

Nicolosi, G. (2019) La migrazione come risorsa simbolica dello storytelling politico. Immaginario emergenziale, discorsi d'odio e media in Italia, [Migration as a symbolic resource of political storytelling. Emergency imagery, hate speech and the media in Italy], *Im@go. A Journal of the Social Imaginary*, (14), 101-123.

Noble, S.U. (2018) *Algorithms of Oppression: How Search Engines Reinforce Racism*. New York, NY: New York University Press

Nogueira, S. (2020) *Intolerância Religiosa*, [Religious Intolerance], 1st ed. São Paulo, SP: Pólen Livros

Oehmichen, C. (2018) Los imaginarios de la alteridad y la construcción del chivo expiatorio: Trump y el racismo antinmigrante, [The imaginaries of alterity and the construction of the scapegoat: Trump and the anti-immigrant racism], *Revista Pueblos y Fronteras Digital*, 13 (e344), 1-21.

Oliva, A.R. (2003) A história da África nos bancos escolares: representações e imprecisões na literatura didática, [The history of Africa in school benches: representations and inaccuracies in textbooks], *Estudos Afro-Asiáticos*, 25 (3), 421-461.

Olmos Alcaraz, A. (2018) Alteridad, migraciones y racismo en redes sociales virtuales: un estudio de caso en Facebook, [Otherness, migrations and racism inside virtural social networks: a case of study on Facebook], *REMHU: Revista Interdisciplinar da Mobilidade Humana*, 26 (53), 41-60.

Oña-Arcentales, K., Alvarado-Angulo, D., Cabrera-Martínez, L. and Ureña-López, R. (2022) Discursos de odio y comunicación violenta ante contenidos de prensa digital en Ecuador, [Hate speeches and violent communication facing digital press content in Ecuador], *Maskana*, 13 (1), 4-13.

Parodi, R., Cuesta, M. and Wegelin, L. (2022) Problematizar los discursos de odio: democracia, redes sociales y esfera pública, [Problematising hate speech: democracy, social networks and publis sphere], *Tram[p]as de la Comunicación y la Cultura*, e061 (87), 1-31.

Pasta, S., Santerini, M., Forzinetti, E. and Della Vedova, M.L. (2021) Antisemitismo e Covid-19 in Twitter. La ricerca dell'odio online tra automatismi e valutazione qualitativa, [Antisemitism and Covid-19 on Twitter. The search for hatred online between automatisms and qualitative evaluation], *Form@re - Open Journal per la formazione in rete*, 21 (3), 288-304.

Paulin, M. and Boon, S.D. (2021) Revenge via social media and relationship contexts: Prevalence and measurement, *Journal of Social and Personal Relationships*, 38 (12), 3692-3712.

Pereira, G.M. (2017) Intolerância e ódio no cibermundo: observações sobre comentários gerados a partir de uma imagem sobre identidade e gênero no Facebook, [Intolerance and hatred in the cyber world: observations on comments generated from an image about identity and gender on Facebook], *Revista Temática*, 13 (1), 1-17.

Peres-Neto, L. and Pereira, G.A. (2019) Ética, liberdade de expressão e discurso de ódio de gênero em sites de redes sociais, [Ethics, freedom of speech and gender-hating speech on social networking sites], *E-Compós*, 22 (1), 1-25.

Pérez Díaz, M. and Aguilar Pérez, M. (2021) #LadyFrijoles: señalamiento, discriminación y estigma de migrantes centroamericanos a través de redes sociales en México, [#Ladyfrijoles: targeting, discrimination and stigma of Central American migrants through social media in Mexico], *Andamios*, 18 (45), 223-243.

Pérez, R. (2017) Racism without Hatred? Racist Humor and the Myth of "Colorblindness", *Sociological Perspectives*, 60 (5), 956-974.

Perú21 (2020) Martha Chávez: 'Vicente Zeballos se hubiera ido a Bolivia porque es una persona con rasgos andinos' [VIDEO]. [Martha Chávez: "Vicente Zeballos would have gone to Bolivia because he is a person with Andean features" [VIDEO]], *Perú 21*, 01 September, Lima, Peru. Available from: https://peru21.pe/politica/martha-chavez-vicente-zeballos-se-hubiera-ido -a-bolivia-porque-como-moqueguano-y-rasgos-andinos-le-podria-ir-mejor -racismo-discriminacion-noticia/

Petry, H. and Nascimento, D.M. (2016) "Tá com dó? Leva pra casa!" Análise dos discursos favoráveis à redução da maioridade penal em rede social, ["Do you Feel Sorry for Him? Then Take him into Your Home!" Analysis of Speeches in Favor of Reducing the Legal Age for Criminal Responsibility in a Social Network], *Psicologia: Ciência e Profissão*, 36 (2), 426-438.

Philips, T. and Downie, A. (2023) Brazil protests: Lula vows to punish 'neo-fascists' after Bolsonaro supporters storm congress, *The Guardian*, 09 January, London, UK. Available from: https://www.theguardian.com/world/2023/jan/

08/jair-bolsonaro-supporters-storm-brazils-presidential-palace-and-supreme-court

Phillips, S. (2007) A brief history of Facebook, *The Guardian*, 25 July, London, UK. Available from: https://www.theguardian.com/technology/2007/jul/25/media.newmedia

Picca, L.H. and Feagin, J.R. (2007) *Two-faced racism: Whites in the backstage and frontstage*. London, UK: Routledge

Poster, M. (2001) *What's the Matter with the Internet?* Saint Paul, MN: University of Minnesota Press

Quadrado, J.C. and Ferreira, E.S. (2020) Ódio e intolerância nas redes sociais digitais, [Hate and intolerance in digital social networks], *Revista Katálysis*, 23 (3), 419-428.

Rafi, M.S. (2020) Language of COVID-19: Discourse of Fear and Sinophobia, *Social Sciences & Humanities Open*, (20), 1-18.

Ray, K. (2023) The History Of Google Search, *Site Centre*, 09 February, Sidney, Australia. Available from: https://www.sitecentre.com.au/blog/history-of-google-search

Raynaud, M., Goutaudier, V., Louis, K., Al-Awadhi, S., Dubourg, Q., Truchot, A., Brousse, R., Saleh, N., Giarraputo, A., Debiais, C., Demir, Z., Certain, A., Tacafred, F., Cortes-Garcia, E., Yanes, S., Dagobert, J., Naser, S., Robin, B., Baily, É., Jouven, X., Reese, P.P. and Loupy, A. (2021) Impact of the COVID-19 pandemic on publication dynamics and non-COVID-19 research production, *BMC Medical Research Methodology*, 21 (255), 1-10.

Rebs, R.R. (2017) O excesso no discurso de ódio dos haters, [The excesses in the hate discourses of haters], *Fórum Linguistico*, 14 (número especial), 2512-2523.

Rebs, R.R. and Ernst, A. (2017) Haters e o discurso de ódio: entendendo a violência em sites de redes sociais, [Haters and hate speech: Understanding the violence on social media], *Diálogo das Letras*, 6 (2), 24-44.

Rega, R. and Lovari, A. (2019) Ripensare il cyberbullismo tra social media e messaggi d'odio. Pratiche, ibridazioni e trattorie di ricerca, [Rethinking cyberbullying between social media and hate speech. Practices, hybridizations and research trends], *Media Education: Studi e Ricerca*, 10 (2), 194-211.

Reyes Vázquez, J.F. and Barrios De La O, M.I. (2019) El comportamiento de los usuarios de Twitter respecto al tema de la Caravana Migrante a través del Sentiment Analysis (SA), 2019, [The behavior of Twitter users regarding the issue of the Migrant Caravan through Sentiment Analysis (SA), 2019], *De Política*, 7 (13), 11-19.

Rheingold, H. (2000) *The Virtual Community: Homesteading on the Electronic Frontier*. Cambridge, MA: MIT Press

Rossini, C., Cruz, F.B. and Doneda, D. (2015) *The Strengths and Weaknesses of the Brazilian Internet Bill of Rights: Examining a Human Rights Framework for the Internet*, Ontario, Canada, Global Commission on Internet Governance. Available from: https://www.cigionline.org/sites/default/files/no19_0.pdf

Rusert, J., Khalid, O., Hong, D., Shafiq, Z. and Srinivasan, P. (2019) No Place to Hide: Inadvertent Location Privacy Leaks on Twitter, *Proceedings on Privacy Enhancing Technologies*, (4), 172-189.

Rushe, D. (2014) WhatsApp: Facebook acquires messaging service in $19bn deal, *The Guardian*, 20 February, London, UK. Available from: https://www.theguardian.com/technology/2014/feb/19/facebook-buys-whatsapp-16bn-deal

Rusli, E.M. (2012) Facebook Buys Instagram for $1 Billion, *The New York Times*, 09 April, New York, NY. Available from: https://archive.nytimes.com/dealbook.nytimes.com/2012/04/09/facebook-buys-instagram-for-1-billion/

Ryan, D. (1999) Colonialism and Hegemony in Latin America: An Introduction, *The International History Review*, 21 (2), 287-296.

Rzepnikowska, A. (2018) Racism and xenophobia experienced by Polish migrants in the UK before and after Brexit vote, *Journal of Ethnic and Migration Studies*, 44 (13), 1-17.

Sánchez-Tarragó, N., Bufrem, L.S. and Macedo Dos Santos, R.N. (2015) La producción científica Latinoamericana desde una mirada poscolonial, [Latinoamerican scientific production from a postcolonial viewpoint], *Tendências da Pesquisa Brasileira em Ciência da Informação*, 8 (2), 182-202.

Santerini, M. (2019) Discorso d'odio sul web e strategie di contrasto, [Hate speech on the web and contrast strategies], *MeTis. Mondi Educativi. Temi, Indagini, Suggestioni*, 9 (2), 51-67.

Schild, L., Ling, C., Blackburn, J., Stringhini, G., Zhang, Y. and Zannettou, S. (2020) "Go eat a bat, Chang!": An Early Look on the Emergence of Sinophobic Behavior on Web Communities in the Face of COVID-19, *Social and Information Network*, 1-16.

Seara, I.R. and Cabral, A.L.T. (2020) Barbarus ad portas: a agressividade verbal em comentários na rede social Facebook, [Barbarus ad portas: the verbal aggression in comments on the social network Facebook], *Comunicação & Sociedade*, 38, 139-160.

Sepúlveda Logorreta, N.P. and Flores Treviño, M.E. (2019) Imaginarios, violencia y sexismo entre cibernautas de tres sitios de noticias de Facebook en México, [Imaginaries, violence and sexism among Internet users within three Facebook news sites in Mexico], *Textos en Proceso*, 5 (2), 61-74.

Shepherd, T., Harvey, A., Jordan, T., Srauy, S. and Miltner, K. (2015) Histories of Hating, *Social Media + Society*, 1 (2), 1-10.

Sherman, N. (2023) Is Elon Musk right to ditch the Twitter bird logo? *BBC News*, 25 July, London, UK. Available from: https://www.bbc.co.uk/news/business-66296468

Silva, D.C.P. (2020a) Performances de gênero e raça no ativismo digital de Geledés: interseccionalidade, posicionamentos interacionais e reflexividade, [Gender and Race Performances in the Digital Activism of Geledés: Intersectionality, Interactional Positions and Reflectivity], *Revista Brasileira de Linguística Aplicada*, 20 (3), 407-442.

Silva, J.M., Oliveira, U.M.C. and Miranda, J.R. (2020) Do discurso de ódio homofóbico à resistência lgbtqia+: uma análise das mensagens publicadas nas redes sociais, [From homophobic hate speech to lgbtqia + resistance: an analysis of messages published on social media], *Revista Relações Sociais*, 3 (4), 1-13.

Silva, L.B. and Aléssio, R.L.S. (2019) Redes de ódio: A homofobia no Facebook, [Hate networks: Homophobia on Facebook], *Estudos & Pesquisas em Psicologia*, 19 (1), 7-27.

Silva, L.R.L. and Botelho-Francisco, R.E. (2020) Gestão de conteúdo de ódio no Facebook: um estudo sobre haters, trolls e naysayers, [Hate management on Facebook: a study about haters, trolls and naysayers], *P2P Inovação*, 6 (edição especial), 38-56.

Silva, L.R.L., Botelho-Francisco, R.E., Oliveira, A.A.A.A. and Pontes, V.R. (2019) A gestão do discurso de ódio nas plataformas de redes sociais digitais: um comparativo entre Facebook, Twitter e Youtube, [The management of hate speech on the platforms of digital social networks: a comparison between Facebook, Twitter and YouTube], *Revista Ibero-Americana de Ciência da Informação*, 12 (2), 470-492.

Silva, L.R.L., Francisco, E.B. and Sampaio, R.C. (2021) Discurso de ódio nas redes sociais digitais: tipos e formas de intolerância na página oficial de Jair Bolsonaro no Facebook, [Hate speech in digital social networks: types and forms of intolerance on Jair Bolsonaro's Facebook page], *Galáxia*, (46), 1-26.

Silva, L.R.L. and Sampaio, R.C. (2017) Impeachment, facebook e discurso de ódio: a incivilidade e o desrespeito nas fanpages das senadoras da república, [Impeachment, facebook and hate speech: incivility and disrespect in the fanpages of senators of the republic], *Esferas*, (10), 95-107.

Silva, M.D.C.G., Lima, S.C.F., Lima, A.F. and Barros, J.P.P. (2022) Necropolítica e vidas não passíveis de luto: a (re)produção midiática do inimigo, [Necropolitics and non-grievable lives: the media (re)production of the enemy], *Psicologia em Estudo*, 27 (e49027), 1-14.

Silva, M.P. and Silva, L.S. (2021) Disseminação de discursos de ódio em comentários de notícias: uma análise a partir de notícias sobre o universo LGBT em cibermeios sul-mato-grossenses no Facebook, [Dissemination of hate speech in news comments: an analysis based on news about the LGBT universe in cyber media from Mato Grosso do Sul on Facebook], *Intercom - Revista Brasileira de Ciências da Comunicação*, 44 (2), 137-155.

Silva, R.G. (2018) Corpos abjetos: a heterossexualidade compulsória e os discursos de ódio nas redes sociais, [Abject bodies: compulsory heterosexuality and hate speech on social media], *Revista Temática*, 14 (6), 126-141.

Silva, T. (2019) *Racismo Algorítmico em Plataformas Digitais: microagressões e discriminação em código*, [Algorithmic Racism on Digital Platforms: Microaggression and Code Discrimination], Paper presented at VI Simpósio Internacional Lavits | Assimestrias e (In)visibilidades: Vigilância, Gênero e Raça, Salvador, BA, 26-28 June. Available from: http://lavits.org/vi-simposio-internacional-lavits-salvador-26_28-de-junho-2019/?lang=pt

Silva, T. (2020b) Visão computacional e racismo algorítmico: branquitude e opacidade no aprendizado de máquina, [Computer vision and algorithmic racism: whiteness and opacity in machine learning], *Revista da ABPN*, 12 (31), 428-448.

Silva, T. (2022) *Racismo algorítmico: inteligência artificial e discriminação nas redes digitais*, [Algorithmic Racism: Artificial Intelligence and Discrimination in Digital Networks]. São Paulo, SP: Edições SESC.

Silveira-Barbosa, P. and Rocha, M. (2018) A (re)execução de Marielle Franco a partir das lentes de O Globo no Twitter, [Marielle Franco's (re) execution from the lens of O Globo on Twitter], *Revista de Estudos Interdisciplinares em Gêneros e Sexualidades*, 1 (10), 51-71.

Slonje, R., Smith, P.K. and Frisén, A. (2013) The nature of cyberbullying, and strategies for prevention, *Computers in Human Behavior*, 29 (1), 26-32.

Smith, P.K., Mahdavi, J., Carvalho, M., Fisher, S., Russel, S. and Tippett, N. (2008) Cyberbullying: its nature and impact in secondary school pupils, *Journal of Child Psychology and Psychiatry*, 49 (4), 376-385.

Society (2016) Internet Governance, *Internet Society*, 26 April, Reston, VA. Available from: http://www.internetsociety.org/what-we-do/internet-issues/internet-governance

Solano Rivera, S. and Ramírez Caro, J. (2019) Nacionalismo, xenofobia y sexismo: El caso del himno nacional Nicaragüense en escuelas Costarricenses, [Nationalism, xenophobia and sexism: the case of the Nicaraguan National Anthem in costarrican schools], *Revista Herencia*, 32 (2), 97-122.

Solomon, B. (2016) Yahoo Sells To Verizon In Saddest $5 Billion Deal In Tech History, *Forbes*, 25 July, New York, NY. Available from: https://www.forbes.com/sites/forbesdigitalcovers/2018/07/12/why-the-rocks-social-media-muscle-made-him-hollywoods-highest-paid-actor/?sh=46310c1b136b

Solon, O. (2017) Ex-Facebook president Sean Parker: site made to exploit human 'vulnerability', *The Guardian*, 09 November, London, UK. Available from: https://www.theguardian.com/technology/2017/nov/09/facebook-sean-parker-vulnerability-brain-psychology

Sorkin, A.R. and Peters, J.W. (2006) Google to Acquire YouTube for $1.65 Billion, *The New York Times*, 09 October, New York, NY. Available from: https://www.nytimes.com/2006/10/09/business/09cnd-deal.html

Southern, M.G. (2023) Google Launches Bard AI Chatbot To Compete With ChatGPT, *Search Engine Journal*, 21 March, London, UK. Available from: https://www.searchenginejournal.com/google-launches-bard-ai-chatbot-to-compete-with-chatgpt/482779/#close

Spallaccia, B. (2018) Nuove virtualità e antica misoginia: sfide e orizzonti per le scienze umane nelle società informatizzate del XXI secolo, [New virtualities and ancient misogyny: challenges and horizons for the human sciences in the computerized societies of the 21st century], *mediAzioni*, (23), 1-14.

Stern, S.J. (1985) Latin America's Colonial History: Invitation to an Agenda, *Latin American Perspectives*, 12 (1), 3-16.

Stocker, P.C. and Dalmaso, S.C. (2016) Uma questão de gênero: ofensas de leitores à Dilma Rousseff no Facebook da Folha, [A gender issue: offenses from readers against Dilma Rousseff on Folha de S. Paulo Facebook], *Revista Estudos Feministas*, 24 (3), 679-690.

Storto, L.J. and Zanardi, R.C. (2019) Análise discursiva de governo coloca ideologia de gênero no ENEM do Pastor Silas Malafaia: discurso político, da natureza e de ódio, [Discursive analysis of government puts gender ideology in ENEM by pastor Silas Malafaia: political, nature and hate speech], *Linguagem em (Dis)curso*, 19 (3), 383-400.

Suart, C., Neuman, K. and Truant, R. (2022) The impact of the COVID-19 pandemic on perceived publication pressure among academic researchers in Canada, *PLoS ONE*, 17 (6), 1-23.

Sullivan, D. (2013) A Eulogy For AltaVista, The Google Of Its Time, *Search Engine Land*, 28 June, New York, NY. Available from: https://searchengineland.com/altavista-eulogy-165366

Taylor, D.B. (2020) How the Coronavirus Pandemic Unfolded: a Timeline, *The New York Times*, 30 June, New York, NY. Available from: https://www.nytimes.com/article/coronavirus-timeline.html

Teles, B.N. (2020) Violência policial e o debate no Twitter em Portugal: o caso do Bairro da Jamaica, [Police violence and the debate on Twitter in Portugal: the case of Jamaica district], *Revista Brasileira de Ciências da Comunicação*, 43 (1), 147-164.

Teso Craviotto, M. and Acevedo, B. (2022) Imaginario social del lema 'refugiado' en las redes sociales de España, [Social imaginary of the slogan 'refugee' in the social networks of Spain], *Discurso & Sociedad*, 16 (1), 88-114.

TGEU (2023) TMM Absolute Numbers (2008 - Sept 2022), *Transgender Europe*, January, Berlin, Germany. Available from: https://transrespect.org/en/map/trans-murder-monitoring/#

Tontodimamma, A., Nissi, E., Sarra, A. and Fontanella, L. (2021) Thirty years of research into hate speech: topics of interest and their evolution, *Scientometrics*, 126, 157-179.

Torbisco Cervantes, Y.S. and Gomero Correa, G. (2021) La opinión pública ante un caso de racismo en redes sociales, el caso de la congresista Martha Chávez [Public opinion in a case of racism in social networks, the case of Congresswoman Martha Chávez], *RISTI - Revista Ibérica de Sistemas e Tecnologias de Informação*, (E46), 137-152.

Torkington, K. and Ribeiro, F.P. (2019) 'What are these people: migrants, immigrants, refugees?': Migrationrelated terminology and representations in Portuguese digital press headlines, *Discourse, Context & Media*, (27), 22-31.

Trindade, L.V.P. (2018) *It is not that funny. Critical analysis of racial ideologies embedded in racialized humour discourses on social media in Brazil*. PhD Thesis, University of Southampton. Sociology, Available from: https://eprints.soton.ac.uk/427249/.

Trindade, L.V.P. (2019) Disparagement humour and gendered racism on social media in Brazil, *Ethnic and Racial Studies*, 43 (15), 2766-2784.

Trindade, L.V.P. (2020a) 'My hair, my crown'. Examining black Brazilian women's anti-racist discursive strategies on social media, *Canadian Journal of Latin American and Caribbean Studies*, 45 (3), 277-296.

Trindade, L.V.P. (2020b) *No Laughing Matter: Race Joking and Resistance in Brazilian Social Media*. Wilmington, DE: Vernon Press

Trindade, L.V.P. (2020c) The silent takeover of power by the far-right, *Annals of Social Sciences & Management Studies*, 5 (1), 5-7.

Trindade, L.V.P. (2022) *Discurso de ódio nas redes sociais*, [Hate Speech on Social Media]. São Paulo, SP: Editora Jandaíra

Trindade, L.V.P. (2023) *Precisamos falar de regulação das plataformas de redes sociais*, [We need to talk about the regulation of social media platforms], IN:

Guilherme, W.D., Augusto, D.L.L. and Mello, R.G. (eds.) Diálogos Interdisciplinares em Ciências Humanas. Rio de Janeiro, RJ: Editora e-Publicar, 178-194.

Trindade, L.V.P. and Acevedo, C.R. (2023) From 'model minority' to outsiders: COVID-19 and the surge of anti-Chinese sentiment, *International Journal of Humanities, Social Science and Management*, 3 (4), 254-265.

Turkle, S. (1995) *Life on the Screen.* New York, NY: Simon and Schuster

UN (2023a) Freedom of speech is not freedom to spread racial hatred on social media: UN experts, *UN News*, 06 January, New York, NY. Available from: https://www.ohchr.org/en/statements/2023/01/freedom-speech-not-freedom-spread-racial-hatred-social-media-un-experts

UN (2023b) 'Urgent need' for more accountability from social media giants to curb hate speech: UN experts, *UN News*, 06 January, New York, NY. Available from: https://news.un.org/en/story/2023/01/1132232

Valdez-Apolo, M.B., Arcila Calderón, C. and Jiménez Amores, J. (2019) El discurso del odio hacia migrantes y refugiados a través del tono y los marcos de los mensajes en Twitter, [Hate speech towards migrants and refugees through the tone and frames of messages on Twitter], *RAE-IC, Revista de la Asociación Española de Investigación de la Comunicación*, 6 (12), 361-384.

van Dijk, T.A. (2005) *Racism and discourse in Spain and Latin America.* New York, NY: John Benjamins Publishing

Vega, J. (2022) Xenofobia, nacionalismo y COVID-19: la construcción del migrante venezolano en el discurso sobre la vacunación en redes sociales, [Xenophobia, nationalism and COVID-19: the construction of the Venezuelan migrant in the discourse on vaccination in social networks], *Lengua y Sociedad*, 21 (11), 129-147.

Vepsä, S. (2021) *Anticipating and Managing the Risks of Online Harassment: Research, Reports, Guides and Recommendations.* Helsink, Finland: IDA – Intiimiys Datavetoisessa Kulttuurissa

Vilicic, F. and Beer, R. (2016) As caretas do Facebook [New Facebook's emojis], *Veja*, Sao Paulo, SP, 9. 02 March, 70-71

Virdee, S. and McGeever, B. (2018) Racism, Crisis, Brexit, *Ethnic and Racial Studies*, 41 (10), 1802-1819.

Vitali, M.M., Castro, A., Caravaca-Morera, J. and Soratto, J. (2019) "Homem é homem e mulher é mulher, o resto, sem-vergonhice": representações sociais da transexualidade sobre comentários da internet, ["A man is a man and a woman is a woman; everything else is hanky-panky": social representations of transsexuality on internet comments], *Saúde e Sociedade*, 28 (4), 243-254.

Vizcaíno-Verdú, A., Contreras-Pulido, P. and Guzmán-Franco, M.D. (2020) Construcción del concepto fanbullying: Revisión crítica del acoso en redes sociales, [Building the fanbullying concept: Critical review of social media harassment], *Pixel-BIT Revista de Medios y Educación*, (57), 211-230.

Wade, P. (2010) *Race and Ethnicity in Latin America.* London, UK: Pluto Press

Wagner, W. (1994) Introduction: aspects of social representation theory, *Social Science Information*, 33 (2), 155-161.

Wainberg, J.A. and Müller, A.A.C. (2017) Eleições 2.0: Ódio nas redes durante a campanha presidencial de 2014, [Elections 2.0: hate on the networks during the race for the presidency in 2014], *Conexão, Comunicação e Cultura*, 16 (31), 43-71.

WEF (2016) The world's movement of people – in one map, *World Economica Forum*, 20 July, New York, NY. Available from: https://www.weforum.org/ agenda/2016/07/the-worlds-immigration-in-one-map/

Wiggers, K. and Sawers, P. (2023) Google's Bard chatbot finally launches in the EU, now supports more than 40 languages, *TechCrunch*, 13 July, London UK. Available from: https://techcrunch.com/2023/07/13/googles-bard-finally-lands-in-the-eu-now-supports-more-than-40-languages/

Wilson, R.E., Gosling, S. and Graham, L.T. (2012) A Review of Facebook Research in the Social Sciences, *Perspectives on Psychological Science*, 7 (3), 203-220.

Xinhua, B. (2022) UN chief warns of online stigma, *Global Times*, 19 June, Beijing, China. Available from: https://www.globaltimes.cn/page/202206/12 68457.shtml

Yoon, I. (2016) Why is it not Just a Joke? Analysis of Internet Memes Associated with Racism and Hidden Ideology of Colorblindness, *Journal of Cultural Research in Art Education*, 33, 92-123.

Zannoni, F. (2017) Razzismo e xenofobia nei social network. La pedagogia interculturale tra tecnologie e nuove emergenze, [Racism and xenophobia in social networks. Intercultural pedagogy between technologies and new emergencies], *Annali Online della Didattica e della Formazione Docente*, 9 (13), 214-229.

Zuban, P. and Rabbia, H.H. (2021) Discursos de odio online hacia los feminismos en Argentina, [Online hate speech towards feminisms in Argentina], *Inclusive: La Revista del INADI*, 2 (3), 25-41.

# Index

# E

# F

# G

# H

# I

# Y

www.ingramcontent.com/pod-product-compliance
Lightning Source LLC
Chambersburg PA
CBHW062042270326
41929CB00014B/2503